VOLUME II

Women in Latin America The 20th Century

by
SUSAN HILL GROSS & MARJORIE WALL BINGHAM

JANET DONALDSON, EDITOR

WOMEN IN WORLD AREA STUDIES

ESEA Title IVC WWAS
St. Louis Park and Robbinsdale Schools

© Copyright 1985

Glenhurst
Publications, Inc.

Publishers of Women's History Curriculum
Central Community Center/6300 Walker St./St. Louis Park, MN 55416/(612) 925-3632

Picture Credits—(Volume II)

Library of Congress Catalog Card Number 84-073429

International Standard Book Numbers
0-914277-07-6 Paper Edition
0-914227-06-8 Library Edition

Acknowledgments

Excerpt from *Signs*, Vol. 5, No. 1 (Autumn 1979), "The Beginnings of the Women's Suffrage Movement in Brazil," by June Hahner, pages 203-204. By permission of The University of Chicago Press, publisher.

Poem from *Bread & Roses*, Vol. 3, No. 1 (Winter 1982), pages 22 and 25. Quoted in, Marjorie Agosin and Sylvia Payne, "The Silent Voices: Poets of Latin America."

Poem from *Nine Latin American Poets*, Rachel Benson, translator, pages 255-257 (New York: Cypress Books and Las Americas Publishing Co., 1968).

Poem from *Ten Notable Women of Latin America*, page 91. Quoted in, James Henderson and Linda Roddy Henderson (Chicago: Nelson-Hall, 1978).

Poems from *Selected Poems of Gabriela Mistral*, translated by Doris Dana. Published for the Library of Congress by Johns Hopkins University Press, Baltimore, Maryland 21218. Copyright 1961, 64, 70, 71 by Doris Dana. Reprinted by permission of Joan Daves.

Excerpts from *Journal of a Voyage to Brazil, and Residence There, During Part of the Years 1821, 1822, 1823*, by Maria Dundas Graham (Lady Maria Calcott) (New York: Frederick A. Praeger, 1969).

Excerpts from *My Mission in Life*, by Eva Perón, pages 60-61 (New York: Vantage Press, 1953).

Excerpts from *MUCIA—Women in Development Network*, pages 97-98, Interim Report of Research on "The Economic Role of Women in Small-Scale Agriculture in the Eastern Caribbean: St. Lucia," by Barbara Knudson and Barbara Yates.

Excerpts from *Women of the Forest*, by Yolanda Murphy and Robert Murphy, pages 68, 122-123. © 1974, Columbia University Press. Reprinted by permission of the publisher.

Excerpts from *Jungle Journey*, by Jo Besse McElveen Waldeck, pages 210-212. Copyright 1946 by Jo Besse McElveen Waldeck. Reprinted by permission of Viking Penguin Inc.

Excerpt from *International Journal of Women's Studies*, Vol. 1, No. 1 (January/February 1978), "The Mother, The Macho and The State," by Joan Myers Weimer, pages 80-81. Published by Eden Press.

Excerpt from *Journal of Inter-American Studies*, Vol. 8 (July 1966), "The Servant Class in a Developing Country: Ecuador," by Emily M. Nett, pages 441-442.

Excerpt from *Latin American Woman: The Meek Speak Out*, edited by June H. Turner. Reprinted with permission of June Haney Turner and International Education Development, Inc. from the article, "Our National Inferiority Complex: A Cause for Violence?" by Ana Audilia Moreira de Campos, El Salvador. Copyright © 1980 by June Haney Turner and International Educational Development, Inc.

Excerpts from *Women and the Ancestors*, by Virginia Kerns (Urbana: University of Illinois Press, 1983).

Newspaper article, "Perón returns to Argentina to greet new rule,"—Minneapolis Star & Tribune and Los Angeles Times. Copyright 1983, Los Angeles Times. Reprinted by permission.

TABLE OF CONTENTS

Introduction

This book, *Women in Latin America*, is meant to enhance regular social studies curriculum units on Latin America. The basic idea of this book, as well as others in the *Women in World Area Studies* series, is that women have led very different lives, depending on factors such as time, place, class, life stage and individual talents. The status of women in the many cultures of the world has varied greatly, as has the status of women within a particular culture.

People in the United States and Europe often have the impression that, historically, the status of women in Latin America has been low. Striking features of Latin American history, however, are the many eminent women and unusual roles for women from pre-Columbian times to the present. These eminent women and unusual roles will be discussed in the book.

The great variety of life styles and opportunities for women is perhaps not so surprising when the great diversity of Latin American countries is considered. People in the United States have a tendency to think that the many countries of Latin America are culturally similar to Mexico because Mexico is the most familiar country to North Americans. Although there are some generalizations that may be true about Latin American culture, it is important to recognize the differences between Latin American peoples and countries.

The following two models may suggest this diversity. First, in United Nations materials, geographic divisions are used which group Latin American countries by climate or region:

Region or Country of
Latin America

MIDDLE AMERICA
Costa Rica
El Salvador
Guatemala
Honduras
Mexico
Nicaragua
Panama

CARIBBEAN
Bahamas
Barbados
Cuba
Dominica
Dominican Republic
Grenada
Haiti
Jamaica
Netherland Antilles
Puerto Rico
St. Lucia
Trinidad and Tobago

TROPICAL SOUTH AMERICA
Bolivia
Brazil
Colombia
Ecuador
Guyana
Paraguay
Peru
Suriname
Venezula

TEMPERATE SOUTH AMERICA
Argentina
Chile
Uruguay

These groupings may remind students of the vast size, climatic range and geographic variations of Latin America.

Another way of grouping Latin American countries has been suggested by Brazilian anthropologist Darcy Ribeiro. He divides the Americas into three groups by the history of their peoples and how they came to have an identifiable culture. The following are Ribeiro's groupings and a brief summary description of each:

THE WITNESS PEOPLES
Mexico
Peru
Ecuador
Bolivia
Middle America

According to Ribeiro, The Witness Peoples are survivors of ancient civilizations such as the Aztec, Maya and Inca that were overrun by European conquerors, especially those of the Spanish. These people have gone through a long process of adapting to Spanish culture but have also imposed their ancient cultural ways on those brought from Europe.

These areas were much more heavily populated than was Spain at the time of the conquests. Their societies were totally different than those of Europe. They had theocratic governments (rule by religious priests), their agrarian (farm) economies depended on irrigation such as those of other ancient civilizations like Mesopotamia, Egypt, China and India.[1]

---

[1]Darcy Ribeiro, *The Americas and Civilization* (New York: E. P. Dutton and Company, Inc., 1971), p. 97.

THE NEW PEOPLES
Brazil
Venezuela
Colombia
Antilles
Chile

The New Peoples were formed by combining groups of people from drastically differing societies, racial groups and areas. These peoples were the blacks brought as slaves from Africa, indigenous peoples already present and Europeans, both Spanish and, in Brazil—Portuguese. The Portuguese and Spanish imposed their language, religion and social order on these other peoples but each group contributed to what is called The New Peoples. These New Peoples were composed of several races but have been intermarrying and unified through language, the same social organizational beliefs and technology.[2]

THE TRANSPLANTED PEOPLES
United States
Canada
Argentina
Uruguay

The Transplanted Peoples are those who came to the open spaces, areas comparatively sparsely populated by indigenous groups which the colonists generally warred against or displaced (rather than living with them). More recent immigrations formed these Transplanted Peoples. In Uruguay and Argentina these were European immigrations particularly of Italians, British and Spanish, to the River Plata area.[3]

Although this is only a brief summary of Ribeiro's three groups, they do perhaps suggest the great differences between areas and countries of Latin America. In reading over the essays in this book, students should keep in mind the great differences between the various areas and countries of Latin America. This diversity is reflected in the great variety of life styles that makes the history of Latin American women both rich and fascinating.

★　　★　　★

VOLUME I:
Women in Latin America—
from Pre-Columbian Times
to the 20th Century

The Women in World Area Studies book, *Women in Latin America— from Pre-Columbian Times to the 20th Century* was the first of two volumes on the history and culture of Latin American women appropriate for secondary students. Like others in the WWAS series, this unit points up the diversity of women's lives, depending on their time, place, class, or individual talents.

Chapter I described something of the lives of women in pre-Columbian Central and South America. The status of women in the Maya, Inca, and Aztec are emphasized. Archaeological finds, works of art, documentations from remaining ancient codices, and early travelers' accounts are among the sources used to describe women's roles and status before the European conquests. An inductive lesson using pre-Columbian art focuses on the

---

[2]*Ibid.*, p. 175-176, p. 189.

[3]*Ibid.*, p. 347-348.

importance of female deities in pre-Columbian religions, and demonstrates some of the difficulties that archaeologists encounter when evaluating artifacts.

The next chapter presented the special problems, sorrows, and adjustments forced on indigenous women by the European conquest of their lands. Some women died as victims of brutality, some acted as mediators between their cultures and those of the Europeans, and some became rebels who fought the conquerors. Individuals who were examples of each of these methods of adjustment are described.

Four cultural themes which have strongly influenced the lives of many women in Latin American history are described in Chapter III. These themes are:
- the strong class system
- the ideals of machismo and marianismo as models for male/female behavior
- the importance of the Roman Catholic Church
- the central position of the family

These cultural realities may explain some of the special opportunities and restrictions that have influenced the lives of women in the history of Latin America.

The final chapter in Volume I, *Women in Latin America—from Pre-Columbian Times to the 20th Century*, dealt with the history of Latin American women in the 19th century. Because few Latin American women were literate, leaving no written records of their own lives, the accounts of travelers to Latin America have been major historical sources for women's history. The observations of outsiders frequently suffer from cultural bias or superficial knowledge of Latin American culture. These problems are discussed. However, many of these accounts were thoughtful, lively descriptions of women that Europeans and North Americans met on their travels to Latin America.

Important roles for 19th century Latin American women were their activities in the wars of independence. The tertulias, or salons, organized by women that fostered revolution, the women spies, the women who acted as quartermater corps to the armies, and women who fought as "Lady Colonels" and as ordinary soldiers are important to the history of Latin American independence. Given the very limited military role of women in most contemporary Latin American countries, their extensive historical involvement in the military is impressive.

The last section tells something of the eminent women of power in 19th century Latin America. Women like Eliza Lynch, Empress Carlotta, and others are discussed. Some less well-known but equally fascinating women of this time period are included as well.

Volume I, then, covers women of many different classes from pre-Columbian times through the break with Spain and Portugal. Volume II covers the 20th century history of Latin American women.

Chapter 5

Women in the Early 20th Century
"Leaders without Movements"

A. Women get the Right to Vote in Latin America

Every country where women have the franchise has a different story on how women got their right to vote. The women's suffrage movement in the United States grew out of the involvement of women, particularly Quaker women, in the movement to abolish slavery. These women began by criticizing injustices done to blacks. They came to realize that, as women, they too, lacked property rights, educational opportunities and personal identities. The suffrage movement in the United States was widespread and generally peaceful, involving women of various classes and religions. In Great Britain, where the press and Parliament tried to ignore the women's suffrage movement, women turned to tactics like mailbox bombing, window smashing and hunger strikes to insist on being recognized. Suffrage in both England and the United States came as a result of organized campaigns by women as well as from a recognition of the importance of the work done by women in World War I. Latin American women (in the over 30 countries involved) gained their suffrage rights in a number of different ways, sometimes with little effort on their part. In the complicated world of Latin American politics, some conservative leaders with no record of being in favor of granting women's civil rights, supported women's right to vote. As will be seen in the article, some feminists who had risked prison to gain rights for women, called for the defeat of measures which would let women vote.

Countries in Latin America can roughly be divided into those countries with active feminist or women's rights groups and those without. Even countries with women's organizations—like Mexico, Chile, Argentina and Brazil—did not necessarily have the grass-roots support from masses of people that was found in the United States. Because of class divisions, early women suffragists in Latin America might be called, as one author put it, *"leaders without movements."*[1] A few professional women in each country who had struggled to get an education generally started these movements. These women often fit a pattern that included one or more of these criteria:

- One of their parents was an immigrant of European background.
- They had studied abroad, either in Europe or in the United States.
- They had participated in international women's organizations.
- They had professional training, often as teachers or doctors and were self-supporting.
- They were from the middle class— neither the upper nor the lower class.

Bertha Lutz, whose father was Swiss and who was educated in Europe, is an example of a Brazilian feminist who fit many of these criteria. Amanda Labarca of Chile, who studied in the United States and who organized the *Reading Circles* of Chile is another.

These movements began, as the *Reading Circles* of Chile suggests, with the primary goal of educating women. In the 19th century, women journalists, like Francisca Senhorinha da Motta Diniz in Brazil[2] and Rita Cetina Gutierrez of Mexico[3] began calling for more education for women but did not yet push for the vote for women. In the 20th century however, more women leaders began to see the need for other rights besides the right to an education. Dr. Alicia Moreau of Argentina wrote a pamphlet called

the "Civil Emancipation of Women" (c. 1917). She said that educational change for a woman should *"be followed by the acquisition of her political rights, and all women would come to hold in society the same complete equality as men."*[4] But these early feminists, in the midst of societies which generally saw women's roles as homebound, tried to suggest that their movement would be for equality but not fit the model of Great Britain or the United States. The following excerpts are from a letter of 1918 by Bertha Lutz which began the women's suffrage campaign in Brazil:

"I [Bertha Lutz] am a Brazilian and during the past seven years I have been studying in Europe. It was with great sorrow that I observed upon my return home the situation you described concerning the lack of...respect for women which one sees here in our capital city. The public treatment of women is painful for them and does little to honor our fellow countrymen. More respect, of course, is accorded a woman among the more cultured sectors; but this is superficial and barely conceals the toleration and

[1]Elsa Mae Chaney, "Women in Latin American Politics: The Case of Peru and Chile," unpublished Ph.D. dissertation, University of Wisconsin, 1971, p. 207.

[2]June Hahner, "The Nineteenth Century Feminist Press and Women's Rights in Brazil," in *Latin American Women*, Asuncion Lavrin (Westport: Greenwood Press, 1978), p. 264.

[3]Anna Macias, *Against All Odds: The Feminist Movement in Mexico to 1940* (Westport: Greenwood Press, 1982), p. 61.

[4]Quoted in, Katherine Dreier, *Five Months in the Argentine*, 1918-1919 (New York: Frederic Fairchild Sherman, 1920), p. 256.

Bertha Lutz—Leader of the Brazilian campaign for women's suffrage

indulgence with which she is treated, as though she were a spoiled child. In this regard, despite all the national progress achieved in recent years, we find ourselves lagging far behind. . . .

"Surely the greatest portion of the responsibility for this unfortunate state of affairs falls to men, in whose hands rest legislation, politics, and all public institutions. But we also are a bit to blame. You cited the words of one of our greatest contemporaries, President Wilson, concerning American women: 'They have shown that they do not differ at all from us in every kind of practical endeavor in which they engage either on their own

behalf or on that of the nation.' These words should serve to guide us, for they reveal the secret to which emancipated women owe their equal footing with men. I was in Europe during the war, and I spent the tragic days preceding the victory in England and France. The women's war effort was admirable and heroic. Some were brokenhearted by the death of a son, husband, father, or brother, and each one was full of anxiety and horror, but with great simplicity and courage they all took the soldiers' places and carried out the hardest jobs of the absent menfolk. They brought a lively intelligence and . . . energy to those tasks, which until now were considered impossible for women. And this heroic example of sacrifice and willpower secured that which all the social and political arguments had failed to accomplish. Today they harvest the fruit of their dedication. Fortunately for our country and for ourselves, we have not been called upon to provide the same proof. But even so we feel that we are worthy of occupying the same position. But how can we obtain it? We should not resign ourselves to being the only subordinates in a world on which liberty smiles. We must become worthy of that position to which we aspire and we must prove that we merit it. Clearly, at present almost everything depends on men. But one of the greatest forces for emancipation and progress lies within our power: the education of women and men. We must educate women so that they can be intellectually equal and be self-disciplined. We must educate men so that they become aware that women are not toys created for their amusement. . .Practical demonstrations are infinitely more valuable than anything else; only they are truly convincing. . . . By achieving first place in a competition, Maria José, [first woman allowed to take a Brazilian civil service examination] has also contributed greatly toward the success of our cause. Finally, all the normal school teachers and other women to whom the nation confides the education of its children prove that there are women of great worth in our country also. . . . [I] propose that we channel all these isolated efforts so that together they comprise a definitive proof of our equality. For this purpose I am proposing the establishment of a league of Brazilian women. I am not proposing an association of 'suffragettes' who would break windows along the street, but, rather, of Brazilians who understand that a woman ought not to live parasitically based on her sex, taking advantage of man's animal instincts, but, rather, be useful, educate herself and her children, and become capable of performing those political responsibilities which the future cannot fail to allot her. Thus, women shall cease to occupy a social position as humiliating for them as it is harmful to men. They shall cease being one of the heavy links that chain our country to the past, and instead, become valuable instruments in the progress of Brazil.

Bertha''[5]

As this letter by Bertha Lutz declares, voting for women was not presented as a radical idea, but one that would create progress in the relationships of women and men.

There were men as well as women who felt this to be the case. The women's rights movement gained support from certain male politicians who genuinely felt that women should have equal rights. One of these men was Salvador Alvarado who took over the governorship of the Yucatan Peninsula after the Mexican Revolution. Alvarado encouraged women's education and changed laws to be more fair. He called a feminist congress in 1916 for an official discussion of women's rights. The conference was a stormy one, with topics ranging from the desirability of the status quo to issues concerning birth control.[6] Alvarado's successor in the Yucatan, Felipe Carrillo Puerto, continued his strong interest in women's rights, proposing the vote for women in state elections.[7] In Brazil, men like Lopes Trovao and Juvenal Lamartine were known for their introduction of suffrage bills and general support of women's rights.[8] Men and women supporters of women's rights were often, at least until the 1950's, a minority in their countries where no movements backed them. But as members of a comparatively well-educated class in

[5]Quoted in, June Hahner, "The Beginnings of the Women's Suffrage Movement in Brazil," *Signs*, Vol. 5, No. 1 (Autumn 1979), p. 203-204.

[6]Macias, *Against All Odds*, p. 70-76.

[7]*Ibid.*, p. 90-91.

[8]June Hahner, "Feminism, Women's Rights and the Suffrage Movement in Brazil, 1850-1932," *Latin American Research Review (1980)*, p. 91, 100.

countries where most people were illiterate, a middle-class minority might have considerable influence. A petition signed by 2000 Brazilian women requesting the vote may not seem comparable to the masses of signatures on women's rights petitions elsewhere. In a country in which only 2.5 million women could even read, the collection of these signatures showed a strong effort by women, and Brazilian President Getulio Vargas recognized their value. In the new constitution adopted in 1934, Brazilian women had the right to vote on the same basis as Brazilian men.[9]

In most countries, however, there were more serious problems involving the issues of women's rights and women's suffrage. Feminists were often caught between two opposing political views. On the one side the conservatives wanted to have Latin American culture stay as it was. On the other side the liberals wanted to have changes made in their societies. In other areas of the world the largest groups of opponents to women's rights had been the conservatives. They tended to fear that changes in women's status and roles might mean the breakup of the home, damaging society. In Latin America, the attitude of machismo affected attitudes toward women's political activities. The idea of women in politics went against the machismo notion that men should be in charge. It also went against the marianismo view that women should stay at home and care for the household.

An Argentine man, Clodomiro Cordero, expressed ideas in 1916 typical of this view:

"Only those men who have stopped being men in the real sense of the word want women to be equal with them, lowering them from the altars where they were placed by men's love to be deposited upon the impure earth. . ."[10]

Other men, like the Mexican Minister of Public Education, Justo Sierra, told women, *"let men fight over political questions. . .you fought the good fight, that of feeling, and form souls, which is better than forming laws."*[11] According to another Mexican man, only *"unattractive women, despairing widows and indignant spinsters"* got involved in social causes.[12]

Women tried to counter these arguments by saying that carrying a baby to the voting place once a year would not seriously disrupt family life. They also argued that if women were so virtuous, it would be a good idea if some of that quality got into politics. The conservative's answer was that women belonged in the home and that men would take care of political affairs for women.

Conservatives in many world areas have often been reluctant to

---

[9]Morris J. Blachman, "Selective Omission and Theoretical Distortion in Studying the Political Activity of Women in Brazil," in *Sex and Class in Latin America*, Jane Nash and Helen Icken Safa, eds. (New York: Praeger, 1976), p. 247.

[10]Quoted in, Nancy Hollander, "Women in the Political Economy of Argentina," unpublished Ph.D. dissertation, University of California, Los Angeles, 1974, p. 140.

[11]Quoted in, Macias, *Against All Odds, p. 15.*

[12]Francisco Bulnes, Quoted in: *Vivian Vallens, Working Women in Mexico During the Porfiriato, 1880-1910* (San Francisco: R & E Research, 1978), p. 222-223.

work for women's rights. But liberals, especially in democratic countries, have been known for advocating rights for women and accepting women's right to vote. In Latin America, however, liberals too, often feared women voting. Women were seen as too tied to the Roman Catholic Church, and therefore, to the old establishment. In Mexico, Catholic women had led boycotts which prevented the closing of Church schools. One nun even instigated the political assassination of Mexican socialist, president-elect Alvero Obregan in 1928. In Uruguay, *The League of Catholic Women* protested against liberal trends between the years 1900 and 1920 by:

- boycotting theater performances of Sarah Bernhardt and Eleanor Duse because their plays dealt with divorced women. Since the papers printed the names of any prominent people seen going to the plays, no one would attend after the League came out against the plays.
- publishing a list of 6500 plays which were not to be read.[13]

The public support that women appeared to be giving the Church plus the conservative ideals of the status quo made liberal leaders reluctant to push for women's rights. The conservatives implied that women who wanted the vote must be "Protestants"—anti-Catholic rebels against the established order.[14] Liberals saw women as tools of the Church, blindly following the established order and not thinking for themselves. Caught between these two opposing views, Latin American women moved slowly to insist upon their right to vote,

although in places like Brazil and Costa Rica, women's movements obtained the franchise for women.

In the 1940's and 1950's an unusual group of "male feminists" appeared in Latin America. These men, with little history of previous interest in women's rights, saw the extension of the vote as a way to improve their own public images—or consolidate their power. Rafael Trujillo, the dictator of the Dominican Republic, had a bad reputation for bilking his country to increase his personal wealth. He hoped to improve his negative image by giving women the right to vote in 1942, suggesting by this that his government was a democracy.[15] Another country which gave the vote to women in the 1940's was Argentina. There had been a fairly strong feminist movement in Argentina. The President, Juan Perón, and Eva Perón, his wife, changed the character of this movement. She stressed the needs of lower-class women whom she saw as loyal to Perónist rule. Juan Perón backed women's suffrage but historians are still unsure whether he was a real male feminist—or was interested in female support solely for his Perónist rule.

---

[13]John O'Hara, "The League of Catholic Women in Uruguay," *Catholic World*, 1921, 11 B, p. 219-221.

[14]Chaney, "Women in Latin American Politics," p. 233. Peruvian women who were called "Protestants" in the 1920's were terribly embarrassed by being thought "anti-Catholic" and somehow influenced by foreigners.

[15]Vivian Mota, "Politics and Feminism in the Dominican Republic: 1931-45 and 1966-74," in June Nash and Helen Icken Safa, eds., *Sex and Class in Latin America*, p. 270.

Conservative governments in the 1950's, like that of General Odria of Peru, suddenly gave women the right to vote, even though there had been no widespread agitation for it. The expectation was that women were more conservative and might support his government.[16] These actions put feminists in a quandary. Victoria Ocampo, writer and supporter of women's rights, opposed the bill for suffrage in Argentina because it came from Perón.[17] Magda Portal, jailed for her radical ideas in Peru, also worried about women's voting and opposed suffrage while conservatives were in power.[18]

By the middle 1950's it became an international embarrassment to be one of the last countries in the world to grant women's suffrage. It might be expected that a dictatorship like Paraguay might hold out until the 1960's, but for a democratic country like Mexico, the lack of women's suffrage seemed odd. In the debate over their suffrage bill, Senator Aquiles Elorduy pointed out that it was a serious embarrassment for Mexico in its international affairs to proclaim human rights and to protest others' rights when half of the adult Mexican population could not vote.[19] Other arguments came from women, reminding leaders that women had paid their dues as soldiers and supporters in the Mexican Revolution. They also pointed out the large group of Mexican women workers who were being taxed (and legislated for) without representation. Women in Mexico voted in their first national election in 1958, and Mexican political leaders like Lopez Mateos worked speedily to gain women's support. As for the fears of women voting strictly for the interests of the Church, that influence did not materialize in these campaigns.[20]

There is no simple explanation of how Latin American women got the right to vote. In some countries, this right came as an unrequested gift, as in Peru. It was the result of organized campaigns in other countries, such as Chile, Brazil and Mexico. But however it came, new women voters owed something to those early feminists—women like Amanda Labarca (Chile), Bertha Lutz (Brazil), Homila Galindo (Mexico), Maria Alvarde Rivera (Peru) and Paulina Luisi (Uruguay). They braved personal insult and gave of their time to help bring the possibility of wider democratic principles to Latin America.

---

[16]Chaney, "Old and New Feminists in Latin America: The Case of Chile and Peru," *Journal of Marriage and the Family*, Vol. 35, No. 2 (May 1973), p. 336.

[17]Hollander, "Women in the Political Economy of Argentina," p. 285.

[18]Chaney, "Women in Latin American Politics: The Case of Peru and Chile," unpublished Ph.D. dissertation, University of Michigan, Ann Arbor, 1971, p. 278.

[19]Ward Morton, *Woman Suffrage in Mexico* (Gainsville, University of Florida, 1962), p.75.

[20]*Ibid.*, p. 111

Points to Consider

1. Look over this list of the years in which selected countries granted National Women's Suffrage— then answer the questions that follow.

New Zealand	1893
Australia	1902
Finland	1906
Norway	1913
Denmark	1915
Iceland	1915
USSR	1917
Canada	1917

(except the province of Quebec, where women could not vote until 1940)

Austria	1918
German Federal Republic	1918

(thirty-six women were elected to the 421-seat National Assembly the following year)

Poland	1918
Belgium	1919
Great Britain	1919
Holland	1919
Ireland	1919
Sweden	1919
United States	1920
Ecuador	1929
Brazil	1932
Uruguay	1932
Cuba	1934
El Salvador	1939
Dominican Republic	1942
Guatemala	1945
France	1945
Japan	1945
Panama	1945
Argentina	1947
Belgium	1947
China (mainland)	1947
Venezuela	1947
Chile	1949
Costa Rica	1949
Haiti	1950
Bolivia	1952
Mexico	1953
Honduras	1955
Nicaragua	1955
Peru	1955
Colombia	1957
Paraguay	1961
Iran	1963
Switzerland	1971

(in federal elections; women were earlier able to vote in canton and local elections)

Portugal	1971

(limited suffrage and right to hold office)

San Marino	1971

(limited suffrage and right to hold office)

Syria	1971

(limited suffrage and right to hold office)

Liechtenstein	1972

Nations that still have not given women full voting rights as of 1980 include Jordan, Kuwait, Saudi Arabia and Yemen. (African nations generally granted both men and women the vote upon achieving independence from colonial powers after World War II).

What things do you notice about the time periods in which various countries extended national voting rights to women?

Does anything about the list surprise you? If so, what? Women's right to vote has been seen as one index of status—in other words—it shows how well off they are in a particular society.

What arguments could be made to support voting rights as an indication of women's status? What arguments could be made to refute (or disagree with) voting rights as an indication of women's status?

Why might being allowed to vote mean little in some countries?

Four small countries still have not fully extended the vote to women. What reasons do you think they might give for not allowing women the vote?

2. What arguments did Latin American conservative politicians give against allowing women to vote? Why did some of these conservatives change their minds and push for women's suffrage?

3. What arguments did liberal politicians give in Latin America against allowing women to vote? What arguments were made for women's suffrage by men like Aquiles Elorduy of Mexico?

4. Elsa Chaney, social scientist and consultant on Latin American women, says of the vote for women:

   "The vote has had great symbolic importance for women in Latin America and served to awaken many to their first awareness of the political process."[21]

   From what you know of the expected roles of women in different classes of Latin America, why might being given the right to vote—even if symbolic—be important to them?

---

[21]Chaney, "Women in Latin American Politics," p. 279.

B. Education for Women
A Controversial Subject

From colonial times to the mid-20th century most women in Latin America could not read nor write.[1] Brazilian women's wills of the 16th and 17th centuries usually were signed by male witnesses. The explanation for this was given in their wills. ***"For she is a woman and does not know how to write."***[2] Latin America was not unique in the 17th century in having illiterate women, but by the 19th century the conclusion of most travelers was that Latin America was more backward than either Europe or the United States in its education of young women. Though there were people who fought for women's education, there were cultural complications which have continued to make education for women controversial.

Reasons Given Against Education for Women

One reason given against educating women has been the cultural characteristic that stressed machismo, in which males feel they must dominate females. Fathers in 18th century Peru feared educating their daughters because they might write love letters and read forbidden, sinful novels.[3] Some Peruvian men in the 1970's illustrate similar fears of women reading. As one Andean woman said, ***"They say the men...prefer to marry women who can't read, because if a man receives a letter or a document from someone and the woman can read it, the woman might cause a***

---

[1]June Hahner, ed., *Women in Latin American History* (Los Angeles: University of California, 1976), p. 3.

[2]Quoted: Heleieth Saffioti, *Women in Class Society* (New York: Monthly Review Press, 1978), p. 142.

[3]Jean Descola, *Daily Life in Colonial Peru, 1710-1820* (London: George Allen and Unwin, 1968), p. 111.

fight... "[4] Latin American men, one observer felt, found it convenient not to have intelligent, questioning wives. ***"[The] men prefer dull wives who they can leave at home and go to look for their amusements elsewhere."*** [5]

Some men in Latin America recognized that women needed some education but felt it should be in the marianismo tradition, focusing women's training on religion and household needs. The curriculum of girls' schools before the mid-1800's emphasized subjects like embroidery, painting, singing and memorizing saints' names. A mother and father boasted that their daughter had led such a sheltered life that she had never read a book.[6] An Argentine woman at the turn of the century was horrified at her daughter's love of learning:

"Whenever she caught the child reading anything serious, which she had somehow smuggled into the house, her mother would cry, 'My dear, put away that horrible book immediately, you will get old and wrinkled before your time and no one will want to marry you.'" [7]

In other words, ***"A girl must be accomplished—but not educated."*** [8] Visitors taken to see the few girls' schools of the 19th century most often commented on the embroidery lessons. Julia Ward Howe, herself an advocate of more education for women, made this comment on a school she saw in Cuba:

"The girls' department seemed quiet enough. Here was going on the eternal task of needlework, to which the sex has been condemned ever since Adam's discovery of his want of wardrobe." [9]

An 18th century Brazilian ordinance set up regulations for education in an orphanage. Tutors were told to take care in ***"teaching the boys to read, write and do sums and the girls to sew, wash and make lace."*** [10]

Besides the idea that the proper curriculum for girls should be focused on homemaking skills, other considerations caused a lack of serious educational opportunities for women. One was money. Males as well as females suffered because of a lack of money for good schools. When money was available, however, it was usually allocated to schools for boys and men. In Panama, for example, the history of schools for girls has been a rather depressing one of schools begun but halted when money grew short. Frequent disruptions in Panama's history—such as financial crises or civil wars—also disrupted the financing of girls' schools, though not those of boys. Then the next generation of women would try once again to organize girls' schools.[11]

---

[4]Susan Bourque and Kay Barbara Warren, *Women of the Andes* (Ann Arbor: University of Michigan Press, 1981), p.195.

[5]Lilo Linke, *Andean Adventure* (London: Hutchinson, 1940), p. 124.

[6]Bertita Harding, *Amazon Throne* (Indianapolis: Bobbs-Merrill, l941), p. 119.

[7]Katherine S. Dreier, *Five Months in the Argentine, 1918-1919* (New York: Frederic Fairchild Sherman, 1920), p. 40.

[8]*Ibid.*, p. 40.

[9]Julia Ward Howe, *A Trip to Cuba* (New York: Negro Universities Press, 1969) (1890), p. 89.

[10]Quoted in, Saffioti, *Women in Class Society*, p. 142.

[11]Mirna M. Perez-Venero, "The Education of Women on the Isthmus of Panama," *Journal of the West*, Vol. 12 (April, 1973), p. 325-334.

Within families of limited resources, boys were sent to school instead of girls. Even Andean peasant women saw their sons' educations as more important than their daughters'. Since men seemed to have greater access to high paying jobs, their education might bring more economic return.[12] A bright young Mexican woman in the 1950's who had won prizes all through school and desired to become a nurse was told by her family that there was no money to educate her. Instead she was expected to work in the family bakery, her work going toward family payment of her less able brother's school fees.[13]

There were other objections to educating women besides economic ones. The Catholic Church originally opposed the creation of secular (non-church related) public schools which might compete with parochial schools run by the Church. It was felt that secular schools also provided a less religious education.[14] Co-educational schools, even at the university level, were sometimes looked upon as creating a dangerous mixing of the sexes. One woman in Venezuela in the 1930's thought of entering a university recently made co-educational:

"Always fond of innovations, I attempted to enroll as a student of chemistry; it was the only department in which I could have found female companions. I talked, argued, studied, prepared myself, and passed my examinations for admission. Mother accompanied me, and I can remember her hands trembling for fear I would fail. I suspect they trembled even more when she learned that I had been accepted! Everything went

Young Cuna teacher of San Blas Island, Panama

smoothly until it came time for my first class. Then a family conference was called to persuade me to give up my absurd ambition.

"'You will lose all standing, attending a man's university,' Aunt Isabel insisted in every tone of voice. She is the social arbiter of the family and is always mixing into matters that do not concern her. 'Your own standing, and your family's, too.'

---

[12]Bourque and Warren, *Women of the Andes*, p. 106.

[13]Helen Miller Bailey, *Santa Cruz of the Etla Hills* (Gainesville: University of Florida Press, 1958), p. 138-139.

[14]Mary O. Cowper, "The Education of Women in Latin America," *South Atlantic Quarterly (1920)*, p. 352.

"Plenty of the others talked the same way. Finally Mother, who knows me best of all and is always ready to help anyone to find himself, said:

"'Listen, child, you know that in our circle it is not thought proper for a girl, especially for one as young as you, to attend the university. It may cause us all embarrassment, and it will mean a lot of difficulty for your father and your brother. However, if you think that that is your vocation and you'll be happy as a chemist, go ahead.'

"'Chemists! Glasses on all day, and hands smelling of all sorts of dreadful messes and explosives,' added Aunt Conchita.

"I announced at last that in view of all that the family would have to suffer, I would renounce my plans."[15]

Besides Church and family pressures, there was also social class opposition to public education. One critic of Latin American education in the 1920's pointed out that the upper class generally had been opposed to all mass education but especially that for girls.[16] One Brazilian woman from that era expressed this point of view. *"What would we do for servants if we educated all the common people?...Education gives foolish ambitions to the working people."*[17] Prejudice against educating lower-class people was made complicated because many Native Americans did not speak Spanish, having kept their own languages. Teachers sent out from urban training schools often became discouraged trying to educate these youngsters, and went back with heightened prejudice against Native Americans who, in their opinion, could not learn. A poor woman of Colombia, Carmen de Rodriquez, had this to say in the 1970's: *"We are the victims of an education geared to make us submit."*[18]

Male Support for Women's Education

Despite the opposition to women's education, there were men who supported the idea that women were both capable of being educated and had a right to receive formal intellectual training. In the absence of academically geared schools in the 19th century, fathers sometimes undertook to educate their daughters personally. Mariano Arosemena's example of teaching his daughters geography and social science was held up as a public example to encourage other Panamanian fathers to teach their daughters too.[19] To suggest what these fathers may have been up against, the following selection gives one Brazilian girl's reaction to her private tutoring by her father in 1893:

"Ever since I was little I've been hearing my father say, 'I must teach this girl English. She's a perfect little English girl, but she can't be one without knowing the language.' He only talked about it

[15]Olga Briceño, *Cocks and Bulls in Caracas* (Boston: Houghton Mifflin, 1945), p. 29.

[16]Cowper, "The Education of Women in Latin America," p. 350.

[17]Clayton Sedgwick Cooper, *The Brazilians and Their Country* (New York: Frederick Stokes, 1917), p. 103.

[18]Latin American and Caribbean Women's Collective, *Slaves of Slaves: The Challenge of Latin American Women* (London: Zed Press, 1977), p. 91.

[19]Perez-Venero, "The Education of Women on the Isthmus of Panama," p. 328.

and then he went off to the mine and forgot all about it. Now that he's teaching English at the high school he said to me, 'Let's begin classes Monday.' Today was Monday and I presented myself for my lesson.

"My father thinks that I have unequalled intelligence. No one can even speak of anyone else's intelligence when he's around without his coming out with the same remark: 'Daughter, if you'd just settle down and study one hour every day, I'd like to see the person who could get ahead of you.' I listen to this the same way I listen when they say I'm pretty...But today I felt I disappointed him and I feel sad about it. What makes my father go on thinking such nonsense? I've never given him the slightest proof of intelligence. I've only received two prizes at school. Just in music and gymnastics. Why does he keep on thinking I'm intelligent? It serves him right!

"Today he began by saying that English is easier than Portuguese because the verbs aren't complicated the way they are in Portuguese; there are very few rules, and everything depends on the pronunciation, and I must have inherited that. We were going to begin by reading a book. He read first. I didn't understand a thing and he said that didn't matter and told me to repeat it. I couldn't. He read it a second time and told me to say that THE the way he wanted. I said it about ten times and he kept saying it wasn't right. I saw it was impossible to get it right and I told him I didn't want to learn English any more; he says it's easier than Portuguese, and

maybe it is for other heads, but not mine. Mine is very hard; English can't get in.

"My father looked at me in amazement and said that we'd try again tomorrow."[20]

Reasons given by men for encouraging women's education varied, but the following statement by the governor of Panama, Juan José Argote, in 1832 is representative:

"I must not conclude my address without first recommending to you very highly and very specially, the construction of schools for girls, of which we have none here [on the Isthmus], when this project should be one of the utmost importance in the area of public instruction, for it is of great interest to society that there be well-instructed matrons, good daughters and wives that combine the nobility of virtue with enlightenment of the mind, thus harmonizing usefulness with beauty. Our boys have no more right than our girls to the use of educational funds, nor is the education of one sex more important than that of the other."[21]

Men in various countries supported education for women, like Isidor Gondra in Mexico, José Miguel Carrera of Chile, and a group called the Positivists in Brazil. Perhaps the best known male defender of women's education was

---

[20]Elizabeth Bishop, tr., *The Diary of Helena Morley* (New York: The Ecco Press, 1957), p. 26-27.

[21]Quoted in, Perez-Venero, "The Education of Women on the Isthmus of Panama," p. 327.

Domingo Faustino Sarmiento of Argentina led the movement for better education for girls and women in Argentina and Chile

Domingo Faustino Sarmiento from Argentina. Sarmiento visited the United States and toured schools with the educators Horace and Mary Mann. He was particularly impressed by the women's education facilities and, with the help of Mary Mann, recruited between 65-70 teachers from the United States to come to teach in Argentina.[22] Later, after he became president of Argentina, he tried to institute more public education for both sexes. His co-educational, non-religious schools were criticized by the Church, and economic and political problems in Argentina hurt the new school system. Sarmiento was exiled to Chile for a time, and he encouraged education for women in Chile as

well. The ripple effect of the teachers brought from the United States who remained in Argentina was seen in the next generation of Argentine teachers and feminists. One United States teacher, Mary Graham, became director of the Normal (teacher training) School of La Plata. She had a definite influence on later leading feminists of Argentina. Feminist Cecelia Grierson was taught by one of these so-called *"daughters of Sarmiento,"* Nicolai de Caprile. Grierson was one of the first women to attend medical school and become a doctor in Argentina.[23]

Women Who Promoted Education For Women

Men in Latin America at times encouraged education for women. They were the only ones with the political rights enabling them to urge adoption of women's education by government assemblies. Nevertheless, women still were deeply involved in promoting the idea that women had a right to an education. Sometimes, as in the case of Juana Manso de Noronha of Argentina, these women were ridiculed and accused of being irreligious and unfeminine.[24] Others, like Amanda Labarca, were at first criticized for urging the idea of women's education but were later rewarded for their efforts. Labarca

[22]Domingo Faustino Sarmiento, *Travels: A Selection* (Washington, D.C: Pan American Union, 1963), p. 240.

[23]Nancy Hollander, "Women in the Political Economy of Argentina, " unpublished Ph.D. dissertation, University of California, Los Angeles, 1974, p. 162-164.

[24]Manon V. Guaglianone, "Women of America, Juana Manso de Noranche, Argentine 1819-75," *Bulletin of the Pan American Union 1939*: Vol. 73, Jan. 1939, p. 726.

helped represent Chile at the United Nations and in 1948 was appointed head of the United Nations section on the condition of women. As a young woman she had studied at Columbia University in New York City (1911-1913) and returned to Chile with ideas to further progressive education for women. In the 19th century a reason frequently given in defense of women's education was that educated women made more intelligent mothers. Instead, Labarca emphasized a woman's right to an education as a necessary part of personal freedom. In her farewell address (c. 1920) to graduating teachers from an educational system she had helped to create, she said:

"I would place above all things respect for your personality; I would want you to be not only good, but also great and free, abundantly free, conscious of your worth and of your future . . . "[25]

Educators like Labarca were joined in their crusade for educational reforms by women journalists and newly organized groups of professional women, many of whom, like Labarca, had been educated abroad.[26]

Women Who Wanted To Be Educated

Not only women from middle or upper-class families were interested in being educated. In a 1907 Sao Paulo, Brazil, declaration, three seamstresses wrote of their long working hours—up to 16 a day—and how little time they had to study:

"We too would like to have leisure time to read or study, for we have little education. If the current situation continues, through our lack of

consciousness, we shall always be mere human machines manipulated at will by the greediest assassins and thieves.

"How can anyone read a book if he or she leaves for work at seven o'clock in the morning and returns home at eleven o'clock at night? We have only eight hours left out of every twenty-four, insufficient time to recuperate our strength and to overcome our exhaustion through sleep! We have no future. Our horizons are bleak. We are born to be exploited and to die in ignorance like animals."[27]

Many poor women saw education as a way out of their economic straits as well as a new way of understanding the world. The following selections are from an oral history of a Nahuatl woman of Mexico, Luz Jimenez. Luz described her feelings in 1905 toward going to school:

"In those days almost nobody wanted to send his children to school because they could not dress well enough. Dirty and in rags, they lived in their huts. The children only ran about in the streets or in the cornfields.

"In the village there was a good lady who knew how to read, and she taught in her home. Parents wanted their children to learn how

---

[25]Quoted in, Catharine Manny Paul, *Amanda Labarca H.: Educator to the Women of Chile* (Cuernavaca, Mexico: CIDOC Cuaderno, 1968), No., p. 7/6-7.

[26]Hahner, "The Nineteenth-Century Feminist Press and Women's Rights in Brazil," in *Latin American Women*, Asuncion Lavrin, ed. (Westport: Greenwood Press, 1978), p. 255-278.

[27]Quoted in, E. Bradrord Burns, *A History of Brazil* (New York: Columbia University Press, 1970), p. 358.

to read; they paid a real, twelve and a half cents a month, for each boy or girl who went to study there.

"The lady's name was Mariquita, and her husband was Mauro Melo. He also taught the children. It was in this school that I learned a few letters and that I learned how to read and write.

"Later my mother told me about how I used to cry because I wanted to go to school. At that time there were not many teachers in the village.

"My mother used to take me by the hand as we went to the market place. But when we passed the teacher's house, we saw the children studying or playing. I used to cry because I wanted to be one of the students too. I cried because I wanted to know what was written on the papers. I was not a big girl; I was seven years old. My mother did not want me to go to school because I was small, and the other children might knock me down and hurt me. But since I kept crying, my father and my mother soon took me over to the teacher's home. Later, when I was older, my parents took me to the big school. But they did not want to accept me." The principal of the school said, 'You had better take this little girl home and not bring her back until a year from now. We will accept her then, when she is older. Right now she will do nothing but cry.'

"'But, sir,' my mother said to the principal, 'I beg you to allow my child to stay. She likes to learn. She already knows a few letters.'

"'How can that be?' the principal said. 'She is still only a

child; she is still very small. But you want me to accept your little daughter.'"[28]

When she was finally allowed to go to school, she was impressed by the teacher's insistence on cleanliness and of the things the principal said about education. She was proud of her own progress, too. *"A great man, Justo Sierra, was the Minister of Education in those times. He was completely devoted to see to the progress of the students in their studies. Every Fifth of May, prizes were awarded—toys and three or four beautiful books. I, Luz, received many things as gifts or prizes— playthings and books. I passed every grade and was given a diploma.*

"Around that year, all the children went to school, some washed but others still dirty.

The principal made all the parents appear before him, and he said, 'If the children continue to come here unwashed, we will have to send them home and they will never get an education. Oh fathers and mothers, what do you say? Will you keep your children clean? Or must they be expelled from school? We, the teachers, want your children to grow up clean. Thus Milpa Alta will be great because the children will know how to read, write, and count. They will also know how to draw things on paper. They will learn good lessons. They are still small, but we want to teach them to be clean. And if you, the

---

[28]Luz Jimenez, *Life and Death in Milpa Alta* (Norman: University of Oklahoma Press, 1972), Fernando Horcasitas, tr., p. 21-23.

parents, are not interested in these things, we, the teachers, are. The boys and girls must learn to live properly. You fathers and mothers, you must answer for them now!'

"'Kind sir,' the parents answered, 'how can you demand that our children go to school clean? Water is scarce here in the village. There is very little water. All we can get is two containers of water every third day.'

"The principal answered, 'I know where water can be obtained. It is just a question of getting up early. By eight o'clock in the morning, you will have returned with the water. The children will have sufficient water to wash their faces, hands, and feet. Thus they will learn to be clean . . .

"'You have heard me, oh fathers and mothers! If at the beginning of next week, a single dirty child is sent to school, we will have to send him home. I beg you to listen to what I am telling you. We are going to turn out children who will become teachers or priests or lawyers. Others may have to find work far away from the village. When they grow to be young people, the girls who have gone to school will not have to become servants—grinding corn, kneading dough for tortillas, slaves of the washboard."[29]

Her own educational career went no further. The Mexican Revolution began in 1913. First the rebel forces of Emiliano Zapata fired upon her school; then Venustiano Carranza's troops caught the school in cross fire. The education of Luz was over.

But the way in which Luz Jiminez remembered the principal's words many years later illustrates how central was the role of educator. This was especially true for female teachers. Though often badly paid, an educated woman appeared before pupils as an expert, creating a new image for which a woman might strive—that of the educated teacher. A woman teacher often took for granted that as a professional she would not only sit with male leaders at town meetings, but would also voice her opinions. A woman anthropologist doing research in Brazil in the 1970's found people somewhat puzzled about how to treat her. She was an outsider, a single woman who broke social customs by going about speaking to men. The villagers finally decided that she was like a "school teacher" and so could be treated as a respectable woman with special privileges.[30]

School teachers were allowed special privileges but often had special responsibilities. María Rosa Arrieta came to teach in a small village in 1931. An American who visited over a number of years described what she knew of Rosita's (María Rosa's) arrival at the village:

"At last in 1931, though, a teacher was to come to Santa Cruz. The people lined up on the wide school steps leading to the porch; this was the first of countless receptions and celebrations that were to take place there. Rockets were ready to be set off, many bottles of

[29]*Ibid.*, p. 103-107.

[30]Neuma Aguiar, "Impact of Industrialization on Women's Work in Northeast Brazil," *Studies in Comparative International Development Summer 1975)*, p. 82.

strawberry pop (no doubt) to be consumed, and small, green corn tamales to be passed around for everybody, once the speechmaking and the welcoming were over. Don Amado was then president, and he stood in front with the council to greet the teacher. A caravan of burros bearing the teacher, her family, and her possessions approached up the trail. Don Amado stepped forward to greet 'the honored ones.'

"A frail, sweet-faced, middle-aged lady got off the second burro. She courteously shook hands with the councilmen, listened to Don Amado's long-winded welcome, quickly turned to greet the older women who stood in the background. She asked about the living quarters which were built into the school, about arrangements for cooking. The women touched her store clothes, her hand bag, inspected the suitcases on the third burro, complimented her on her 'pretty young daughter,' a girl of sixteen or seventeen who still sat astride burro number one.

"Then Don Amado asked the lady to make a speech, to tell her plans for organizing the classes, her program for the first week, the costs of the necessary materials. There followed a long hushed silence. Don Amado looked hopefully at the lady; she looked at him in bewilderment. All the members of the council, and the families behind them, stood waiting eagerly, for the whole community loves long, formal speeches. Now it was the teacher's turn.

"Suddenly the guest herself sensed the mistake. She left the group, walked over to the first burro, helped its rider down, and led her by the hand to greet Don Amado. The pretty daughter Rosita, the sixteen-year-old girl and not the middle-aged lady, was the teacher. Rosita's mother, Doña Rafaela, her advisor, companion, and dependent, had come along merely to keep house for her and to watch over her. If Rosita had a long speech ready to make that day, I never heard about it."[31]

Rosita became so important to the people of the village that for the next 30 years—even after she moved away—she acted as the villagers' contact with the outside world. Visitors stayed at her house. She wrote letters to the government to straighten out problems of the villagers. She helped settle their quarrels. The teacher, then, became a centralizing woman like the centralizers mentioned earlier, who organized families but also dealt with the outside world.

In the Barbados Islands teachers are referred to as one of the "poor greats." The term means to suggest that the occupation of teaching offers enough financial security so that an ambitious young person can get out of poverty, even if it does not offer wealth.[32] But it also serves to suggest the prestige given a person with an education in a society in which there are few educated people.

By the 1930's some primary

[31]Bailey, Santa Cruz of the Etla Hills, p. 138-139.

[32]Constance Sutton and Susan Makiesky-Brown, "Social Inequality and Social Status in Barbados," in Sexual Stratification, Alice Schlegel, ed. (New York: Columbia Press, 1977), p. 304.

Barbados school girls

education was available for women in most Latin American countries. Primary schools, largely staffed by women teachers, resulted in a new group of educated women who became a part of Latin American societies. Out of these early teachers' groups came support for feminist movements in Brazil, Chile, Argentina, Mexico and elsewhere. Several major women writers, like Nobel Prize winner Gabriela Mistral, began their careers as teachers. Nevertheless, as a result of both sex and class discrimination, education is not equally available to everyone in Latin America. In a plea for women teachers to teach rural women, Francisca Ramirez of Honduras in the 1970's stated, *"Education, or the lack of it, divides our nation."*[33] It has also divided the sexes in Latin America.

Women are still not equally represented in higher education, for example. Yet, other reformers, including Domingo Sarmiento and Amanda Labarca, were dedicated to education for women and have helped make the division less severe than in the days when few women could read nor write.

★   ★   ★

Points to Consider

1. What were the major reasons given for not educating women in Latin America? Do you think these reasons might be used today for not educating women—not only in Latin America but in other societies as well?

2. Maria Josefa was a major figure in the conspiracies leading to the Mexican Wars of Independence. She was responsible for communications among the members of her group of conspirators. Yet she had a unique problem:
   "While Maria Josefa kept her co-conspirators informed, her messages were a little unusual. She knew how to read, but not how to write, a not uncommon phenomenon considering the emphasis placed on reading rather than writing by the **Colegio Real de San Ignacio.** *As was noted earlier, the older students at the* **Colegio** *read religious works to the younger*

---

[33]Quoted in, June Turner, ed., *Latin American Woman: The Meek Speak Out* (Silver Spring: International Educational Development, Inc., 1980), p. 109.

girls as they went about their daily tasks. As a result, while it is possible that Maria Josefa was quite adept at reading, her writing skills may have been sadly deficient. Given this situation, it was necessary for her to devise a way to send the latest information to her cohorts. It was fairly easy for her to find the correct words in old papers belonging to her husband and which she saved for that purpose. All she had to do then was cut out the appropriate words, paste them on a porcelain plate, and give it to the woman whose responsibility it was to deliver the messages to the next link in the conspiratorial chain.''[34]

Why might the men who had been involved in revolutionary wars indicate a need for women's education following independence from Spain and Portugal?

3. What were some difficult barriers that women had to overcome to become teachers? Why do you think women school teachers were treated differently than other single women in villages?

4. What specific things did Luz Jiminez like about going to school? What things did she find surprising?

See chart, on opposite page

5. Look over the United Nations Chart on Education:
   What things do you notice about illiteracy in Latin America compared with:
   • the world?
   • other world areas listed here (Asia, Africa, Arab States)?

What things do you notice about higher education for women on secondary and university levels when compared with other areas?

Do you think the United Nations statement on school subjects might be true for Latin America? Why?

How might the strong class consciousness in Latin America affect literacy rates? Do you think certain groups have less chance for an education?

Thinking back upon the reading, how did class consciousness affect women's education in both upper classes and lower classes?

---

[34]Janet Kentner, ''The Socio-Political Role of Women in the Mexican Wars of Independence, 1810-1821,'' unpublished Ph.D. dissertation, Loyola University, Chicago, 1975, p. 53-54.

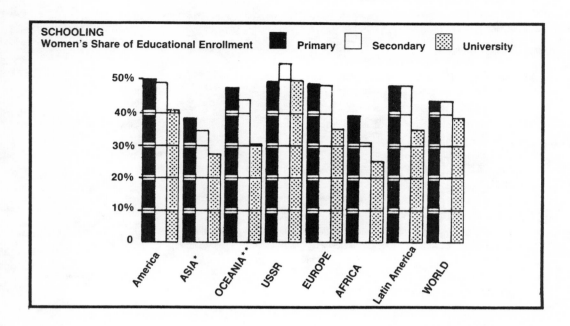

SCHOOLING
Women's Share of Educational Enrollment   ■ Primary   □ Secondary   ▨ University

SCHOOL SUBJECTS
Many schools still have 'girls' subjects' and 'boys' subjects' In most countries:

boys do woodwork and metal work

. . . girls do home science and needlework

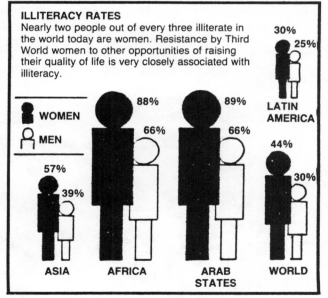

ILLITERACY RATES
Nearly two people out of every three illiterate in the world today are women. Resistance by Third World women to other opportunities of raising their quality of life is very closely associated with illiteracy.

WOMEN
MEN

ASIA   57%   39%
AFRICA   88%   66%
ARAB STATES   89%   66%
LATIN AMERICA   30%   25%
WORLD   44%   30%

Peter Sullivan Sunday Times (London)

* Asia—Excluding China, N. Korea and N. Vietnam

** Oceania—Including Australia, Fiji, New Zealand, Papua New Guinea and Samoa

C. Women Writers— From Anonymity to The Nobel Prize

In 1934 a reviewer of Puerto Rican literature included this description in his discussion of local writers:

"The other is a young woman whose work reveals unusual originality, charm and power, but whose name I am not privileged to give. I can only say, in evidence of good faith, that personally acquainted with her poems and reading them in manuscript, with increasing delight, over a period of years, I would stake my reputation as a critic on their merit. This woman, still in her early thirties, is married to an Hispanic gentleman, of the old school, himself cultured, brilliant and delightful, who believes that for a woman of birth and position to write, and what is worse, to publish her writings, is nothing short of disgraceful. His wife does write, and her manuscript is one woman's authentic footnotes to life; but she has never published one of her poems, nor read them to more than a chosen handful of people. The notable fact is that she continues to write them, with increasing power and maturing technique."[1]

This description highlights two major points about Latin American women writers. First, that women who wished to become writers often faced strong opposition and second, that they created literature despite frequent opposition.

Opposition to women authors took various forms, depending on the time and place in which they wrote, as well as their subject. In 1743, for example, the Prioress of the Convent of Santa Catalina in Peru put on a play she had written for the public. This was acceptable because it

---

[1] Muna Lee, "Puerto Rican Women Writers: The Record of One Hundred Years," *Books Abroad* (1934), p. 9.

contained pious views approved of by the Church.[2] However, when the nun, Sor Juana Inés de la Cruz, criticized a priest's writings, she was censored and threatened with an investigation by the Inquisition. The opinions of other women writers, like Clorinda Matto de Turner, a Peruvian novelist and publisher of the late 1800's, were judged too radical. Her novels criticized both the government's policies and the Church's policies against indigenous peoples. Clorinda Matto de Turner's printing press was destroyed in an attack on her house, and she was exiled to Argentina.[3] Victoria Ocampo, an Argentine publisher and writer during the Peronist era, was arrested and imprisoned for her ideas, as was Juane Belen Botierrez de Mendoza who criticized the Diaz regime in Mexico.

Male writers were also subject to arrest and exile, but sometimes women writers were singled out as special examples. Unlike men, women faced social pressures against their having literary careers at all. Pressure sometimes came from within their own families, as in the case of the Puerto Rican woman whose husband was quoted earlier. The 19th century Cuban poet, Gertrudiz Gomez de Avellaneda, rebelled against her family and lived most of her life in Europe.[4] Even when families approved of their writing, women who tried to combine writing and family life had to deal with the common attitude that their work was unimportant. Elena Poniatowska, a contemporary Mexican writer with children and husband as well as her career, described these views:

"For example, my friends phone and always ask, 'Is madam busy?'

Then, if the servant says, 'She's writing,' they say, 'Oh! Tell her to come to the phone.' But if the servant were to say, 'She's taking a bath' or 'She's in the kitchen preparing a dessert,' then they'd say, 'I'll call back later.' But if I'm just writing, that doesn't matter to anybody, it doesn't impress anybody, and I have to go to the phone immediately. Apparently, they don't consider it an interruption. In fact, it's an absolute lack of respect for the woman writer. They imagine that a woman is just writing her memoirs or perhaps a stupid letter to a girlfriend or that what she has to say can't be important to anybody except to herself, and so is of little consequence. It's a very tough battle, terrifying and tragic."[5]

Particularly if the content of their writing was seen to be too frank, women authors were sometimes viewed as immoral women by their society. The Colombian novelist Fanny Buitrago explained:

"Yes, I've confronted violent reactions, not only against my books, but against myself as a person. Everyone expects extraordinary things of a writer. They expect you to know about philosophy, about new literary

---

[2]Jean Descola, *Daily Life in Colonial Peru, 1710-1820* (London: George Allen and Unwin, 1968), p. 24.

[3]Lucia Fox-Lockert, *Women Novelists in Spain and Spanish America* (Metuchen, New Jersey: The Scarecrow Press, 1979), p. 138.

[4]Beth Miller, "Avellaneda, Nineteenth Century Feminist," *Revista/Review Interamericana*, Vol. 7 (Summer 1972), p. 177.

[5]Quoted in, Beth Miller, "Interview With Elena Poniatowska," *Latin American Literary Review*, Vol. 4 (Fall-Winter, 1975), p. 77.

tendencies, about gymnastics, economics, didacticism. All of this is completely absurd. Besides, in this case, one sees the tendency to think the writer has to be a kind of walking library, and in this country no one has been able to distinguish literature from reality. So they think you must necessarily have experienced what you write. If I write a violent love scene in a book, it is assumed I've experienced all this, and it happens I just haven't had time yet. What can we do? I haven't lived all these experiences—if I'm writing about an assassination, then supposedly I must have seen who knows how many assassinations. So everybody demands explanations. Everyone feels superior, a complete stranger on the street will harass you, or insult you, or perhaps become overly friendly to you. Well, in the final analysis it's a little unpleasant being a woman writer in this country. It's best to go out only from time to time because otherwise they'll eat you alive."[6]

Additionally, financial pressures have been used against women writers. Some usual sources of income for writers were closed to women. Cuba had an academy for writers in the 19th century, and if elected to the academy, writers could apply for government grants. Gertrudiz Gomez de Avellaneda was turned down because she was a woman even though she was world famous. As a writer, Avellaneda found being a woman an *"eternal obstacle."*[7] Women journalists also found they were not always taken seriously. Poniatowska described how her editors first saw her:

"Later they gave me raises. At first they said, 'That girl isn't serious, let's see if she has the spirit to continue for a month.' They seemed to think I was doing it just for pleasure. As they got to know me they said: 'Let's see how long she can last.' Then when they saw that I was very serious about my work, that I was sticking to it and all that, they began to pay me better. At the end they paid thirty dollars an article, twenty-eight after deductions. Then I changed jobs. I had begun working at Excelsior, which is the best there is now in Mexico, but then I went to Novedades, where I've stayed for almost twenty years."[8]

Even Latin American women writers who became famous and respected for their craft had serious problems. At times they did receive special recognition. Gabriela Mistral was a special ambassador from Chile, first, to the League of Nations and later, to the United Nations. Both Rosario Castellanos of Mexico and Carmen Naranjo of Costa Rica were selected to represent their governments as ambassadors to Israel when Golda Meier was Prime Minister. Gabriela Mistral had the unique privilege of being the first Latin American writer to be selected for the Nobel Prize for literature. Yet, the lives of some of the best women writers were unhappy ones. Some,

[6]Raymond Williams, "An Interview With Women Writers in Colombia," in *Latin American Women Writers: Yesterday and Today,* Charles Tatum, ed. (Pittsburgh: Carnegie Mellon, 1975), p. 158.

[7]Miller, "Avellaneda, Nineteenth Century Feminist," p. 181.

[8]Linda Gould Levine, "Maria Luisa Bombal from a Feminist Perspective, from *Latin American Literary Review,* Vol. 4 (Fall-Winter, 1975), p. 152.

like Gabriela Mistral, were forced to live away from their own country. Alfonsina Storni, Alexandra Pizarnik and Violeta Parra all committed suicide. The Uruguayan poet Delmira Agustini was murdered. Maria Luisa Bombal first contemplated suicide, then shot a male friend—who recovered and did not file charges.[9]

Although Latin American women writers are not unique in facing problems of strain and sensitivity, they may have faced unusual pressures.[10] The Costa Rican writer Carmen Naranjo explained what she thought of the pressures:

"What I can say specifically of women's position in our societies is that, from the moment a woman is outstanding, she is expected to act as a circus performer. Acrobatics, clowning, everything is expected. Why? Because there are so few women who are able to stand out. That is, women's social participation is so sporadic, that out of these sporadic appearances they are forced to do wonders or to make fools of themselves. If you do things more or less well, you get a little applause, but if you do something wrong, you fall all the way to hell, and you come very near your death. You do not even have to commit suicide, you are socially and personally annihilated. The only thing that can save you from all this is being sustained by someone, by love. Because you are in the forefront, everything you do is criticized. Take Rosario Castellanos. Even though she already had several excellent novels and poems published, even though she accepted a political and social engagement toward people, she
was greatly criticized for taking the post as ambassador to Israel. . . .
"And if it had been a man, people would have found it natural that she should have taken a post as ambassador. Men get thousands of cultural opportunities, and no one thinks twice about their accepting them. But with women, we are not expected to advance. This is what women must be very conscious of. And now is a difficult period in Latin America for women who want to do things and to change them."[11]

The desire to help further reforms—to change things—may lie behind the drive that makes Latin American women write, even though they face so many obstacles. For although the pressures on these women writers have been considerable, there has also been a substantial body of literature produced by Latin American women. Many of the novels and poems include social criticisms as part of their themes. At times this criticism is directed toward a class society; the novels of Rosario Castellanos and Magdelena Mondragan of Mexico and Clorinda Matto de Turner of Peru have all tried to present a sympathetic view of Native Americans. In the 19th century Gertrudiz Gomez de Avellaneda, the first woman novelist in Latin

---

[9]Beth Miller, "Interview With Elena Poniatowska," *Latin American Literary Review*, Vol. 4 (Fall-Winter, 1975), p. 77.

[10]Writers in the United States who committed suicide include Hart Crane, Ernest Hemingway and Sylvia Plath.

[11]Lourdes Arizpe, "Interview with Carmen Naranjo: Women in Latin American Literature," *Signs*, Vol. 5, No. 1 (Autumn 1979), p. 106.

America, wrote the novel *Sab* about slavery and its evils. Poets of today, like Claribel Alegria and Gioconda Belli, opposed the Somoza government in Nicaragua which eventually was overthrown in 1979, and both have been part of the new revolutionary Sandinista government that replaced the Somoza dictatorship.[12]

Writing was another way of protesting against restrictions placed upon women. Many of the plot themes of women's novels revolve around women who break out of old patterns. The frustrations of women allowed few life choices is another common theme. Writers often protested against customs that treated women unfairly or discriminated against them. In the novel *Herencia*, Clorinda Matto de Turner has a character speak out against the commonly accepted double standard where men—even married men—were allowed sexual as well as social freedoms while women's freedoms were severely restricted:

"Are we living in times when the men are honest? What kind of an example do they set for us? What help do they offer to others. . . . Don't they all have a mistress around the corner? Don't they all chase after velvet and silks, not even bothering to wonder if these silks and velvet are impregnated with the odor of others?. . . That is how it is, for the girlfriend is all the kindness and indulgence while the wife gets the housework, the responsibility for the family name and all of the gossip associated with that position."[13]

Another issue was presented in Silvina Bullrich's autobiography. She

Silvina Bullrich—author of popular best sellers

makes the point that her mother never came to terms with the fact that she had had three daughters and no son. Because girl children were not as highly valued, her mother felt herself a failure. Even though Silvina became a noted writer, none of Silvina's accomplishments could make up for the fact that she was not a boy in her mother's mind.[14] A character in her novel *Mañana digo basta* [I Will Rebel Tomorrow] expressed this view:

"'A girl!' exclaims the doctor, nurse and father, all with resignation. 'Well, the next one will be a boy.' Why didn't anyone say, 'Perhaps this girl will become another Madame Curie, or do

[12]Electa Arenal, "Two Poets of the Sandinista Struggle," *Feminist Studies*, Vol. 7, No. 1 (Spring 1981), p. 19-37.

[13]Quoted in, Fox-Lockert, p. 12.

[14]Corina Mathieu, "Argentine Women in the Novels of Silvina Bullrich," in *Latin American Women Writers: Yesterday and Today*, Charles Tatum, ed., p. 69.

something for humanity like Florence Nightingale, or perhaps a great artist?..."[15]

The sense that women were destined for marriage—not careers such as those of a Marie Curie or Florence Nightingale—is one that appears in many of these novels. Teresa de la Parra was an early 20th century Venezuelan author who did not marry. She explored the feeling that many women had of being trapped because of their sex. One of her characters exclaims:

"If only I had been born a man. Then, Uncle Pancho, you would see what a good time I would have and how I would mind grandmother and Aunt Clara. But, alas, I am a woman, and to be a woman is the same as being a caged bird. They lock you in a cage, they take care of you, they feed you and never let you out while all the rest are happily flying all over. How horrible it is to be a woman! How horrible! Horrible."[16]

The feeling of women being torn between accepting some of their culture's values and rejecting others are themes in the works of two famous, though contrasting, Latin American women poets. These two poets—Gabriela Mistral and Alfonsina Storni—were both concerned with women's roles. Mistral saw women primarily as mothers, though she herself never married or had children. Storni, on the other hand, rebelled against the traditional Latin view of women as saintly mothers while strongly criticizing the double standard.

Gabriela Mistral (1889-1957) was born into a poor Chilean family. When she was three her father deserted them, although he occasionally drifted back for brief

Gabriela Mistral Receiving Nobel Prize for Literature— Photo Courtesy of Doris Dana

Gabriela Mistral receiving Nobel Prize for Literature from the King of Sweden

periods. Her mother became the sole economic and emotional support for Gabriela. Gabriela became a teacher, her verses won prizes, her highest achievement being the Nobel Prize for Literature in 1945. The theme of the suffering yet creative mother stems not only from her feelings for her own mother but also for other poor women. In a *"poet's note"* at the beginning of her volume *Poems for Mothers* she wrote:

"One afternoon, walking through a poor street in Temuco, I saw a quite ordinary woman sitting in the doorway of her hut. She was approaching childbirth, and her face was heavy with pain. A man came by and flung at her an ugly phrase that made her

---

[15]Quoted in, Fox-Lockert, *Women Novelists in Spain and Spanish America*, p. 16.

[16]*Ibid.*, p. 161.

blush. At that moment I felt toward her all the solidarity of our sex, the infinite pity of one woman for another, and I passed on thinking, 'One of us must proclaim (since men have not done so) the sacredness of this...condition. If the mission of art is to beautify all in an immensity of pity, why have we not, in the eyes of the impure, purified this?' So I wrote these poems with an almost religious meaning.

"Some women who, because of high social standing, feel it necessary to close their eyes to cruel but inevitable realities, have made of their poems a vile commentary—which saddened me for their sakes. They even went so far as to insinuate that they should be dropped from my book....No! Here they remain, dedicated to those women capable of seeing that the sacredness of life begins with maternity which is, in itself, holy. They will understand the deep tenderness with which the woman who cares for the children of others, looks upon the mothers of all the children in the world."[17]

The poems by Gabriela Mistral in that volume and others show the respect the poet had for the mystery of giving life and for the concerns of motherhood:

The Sad Mother

Sleep, sleep, my infant lord,
without fear or trembling at my
*   breast,*
though my soul may never
*   slumber,*
though my soul may never rest.

Sleep, sleep, and in the night
sleep more silently

than a single blade of grass ,
a silken strand of fleece.

In you, my fear, my trembling,
let my body sleep.
Let my eyes close on you,
in you my heart find rest![18]

Fear

I don't want them to turn
my little girl into a swallow.
She would fly far away into the
*   sky*
and never fly again to my straw
*   bed,*
or she would nest in the eaves
where I could not comb her hair.
I don't want them to turn
my little girl into a swallow.

I don't want them to make
my little girl a princess.
In tiny golden slippers
how could she play on the
*   meadow?*
And when night came, no longer
would she sleep at my side.
I don't want them to make
my little girl a princess.

And even less do I want them
one day to make her queen.
They would put her on a throne
where I could not go to see her.
And when nighttime came
I could never rock her...
I don't want them to make
my little girl a queen![19]

---

[17]Quoted in, *Nobel Prize Library* (New York: Alexis Gregory, 1971), p. 182.

[18]Doris Dana, tr., *Selected Poems of Gabriela Mistral* (Baltimore: Published for the Library of Congress by Johns Hopkins University Press, 1971) p. 47.

[19]*Ibid.*, p. 69.

★　★　★

Alfonsina Storni (1892-1938) of Argentina was another important Latin American poet. She, like Mistral, began her career as a teacher. She later worked as a writer for children's theatrical companies. Like Mistral, Storni did not marry, although she had a son. This son later wrote that what he remembered most about his mother was her love of truth.[20] This need for truth often led to a frankness, particularly in the area of sexual relations, which went against the polite—at times hypocritical—society of her day. Here is her protest poem about the double standard which demanded that women be sexually chaste—or, as she says, white—while it was all right for men to be sensual.

You Would Have Me White

You would have me white,
You want me to be foam,
You want me to be pearl.
To be a lily chaste
Above all others.
With subdued perfume.
Closed corolla.*

Nor should a moonbeam
Have filtered in to me.
Nor may a daisy
Call herself my sister.
You want me spotless,
You want me pure,
You want me snow white.

You who have held all
Goblets in your hand,
Your lips stained purple
With fruits and honey.
You who at the banquet,
Covered with vine leaves,

Neglected the meat
In feasting to Bacchus.
You who dressed in red
Sped to Ruin
In the black
Gardens of Envy.

You who keep
Your skeleton intact—
By what miracles
I still don't know—
You seek to have me pure
(God forgive you),
To have me chaste
(God forgive you),
To have me snow white!

Flee to the woods;
Go to the mountain;
Wash out your mouth;
Live with the shepherds;
Touch the damp earth
With your hands;
Feed your body
On bitter rice;
Drink from the rocks;
Sleep upon frost;
Renew your tissues
With saltpeter and water;
Speak with the birds
And rise at dawn
And when your flesh
Has altered,
And when you have put into it
The soul
That you left entangled
In bedrooms,
Then my good man,
You may seek to have me white
To have me pure,
To have me chaste.[21]

---

[20]Rachel Benson, tr., *Nine Latin American Poets* (New York: Cypress Books, 1968), p. 252.

* Internal leaves of a flower

[21]*Ibid.*, p. 255-257.

Storni was also concerned with a cage image as a symbol of women's restrictions such as in the poem *Little Man/Little Man, set free your canary who wants to fly away.* This poem, written in 1916, illustrates both her anger and defiance toward the social norms of her time:

I am like the she-wolf
Cut off from the pack
And I went to the mountain
Weary of the plains.
I have a son, fruit of love, love
*   without law,*
Let me not be like the rest, a herd
*   of oxen.* [22]

Storni's verses are often seen in contrast to those of Gabriela Mistral's in the angry and independent frankness of the poetry. Mistral seems to limit women to one role, that of the ever-enduring, suffering mother, while Storni calls for rebellion against women's single role. Yet in one major way—that of trying to gain respect for women— the messages of both poets are similar. These women writers' ideas have been central to cultural discussions of what new directions women should take.

★   ★   ★

Points to Consider

1. What barriers and opposition did women face in becoming writers?
2. What were some of the reasons that women persisted in their writing against opposition?

3. Explain what is meant by the sexual "double standard." Find two examples in the chapter of selections from novels or poems that refer to the double standard. Now select a few lines from the excerpts that tell how the author felt about the double standard. Briefly explain what you think the author was specifically protesting in the lines you selected.
4. In 17th century colonial times, the nun, Sor Juana Inés de la Cruz, wrote a poem complaining about the unfairness to women of the sexual double standard. In the last two stanzas of the poem it reads:

Whose is the greater guilt,
In a sinful passion,
She who falls to his lure
Or he who, fallen, lures her?

Or which is more rightly to be
*   reproached,*
Although both are guilty
She who sins for pay,
Or he who pays to sin? [23]

What did she see as particularly unfair about this double standard? What does she mean by the last two lines? Why might a person who devotes her life to religion— has taken vows of chastity— be interested in this theme? The theme of the double standard has reoccurred in the writing of Latin American women writers from the 17th to the 20th centuries. From what you know

[22]Quoted in, Marjorie Agosin and Sylvia Payne, "The Silent Voices: Poets of Latin America," *Bread and Roses*, Vol. 3, No. 1 (Winter 1982), p. 22.

[23]Quoted in, James D. Henderson and Linda Roddy Henderson, *Ten Notable Women of Latin America* (Chicago: Nelson-Hall, 1978), p. 91.

of Latin American culture, why do you think this has been a major theme?

5. Find examples of two other major themes of Latin American women writers. Do you think these are ones of special concern to women writers? Why or why not?

6. The small country of Uruguay in southern South America has been noted for its many women poets. The Chilean Gabriela Mistral said, *"We women who write in Spanish America feel we own a sort of Uruguayan citizenship card. . . . "*[24] These modern Uruguayan poets include:
Maria Eugenia Vaz Ferreira
Esther de Caceres
Delmira Agustini
Juana de Ibarbouron
Concepcion Silva Belinzon
Clara Silva
Dora Isella Russel

In contrast with many Latin American countries, Uruguay:
• has a population primarily of European origin—with few remaining indigenous peoples.
• at least until recently, has been economically well off and politically stable.
• has one of the highest literacy rates for women in South America.

Why might each of these factors have encouraged women poets? How might they have been role models for each other? (Concepcion Belinzon and Clara Silva are sisters.)

Delmira Agustini (1886-1914) died tragically at 28—murdered by her husband who then committed suicide. The following

poem by Delmira Agustini is in both Spanish and English.

Desde lejos

En el silencio siento pasar hora tras hora,
Como un cortejo lento, acompasado y frío. . . ;
!Ah! Cuando tú estás lejos mi vida toda llora
Y al rumor de tus pasos hasta en sueños sonrío.

Yo sé que volverás, que brillará otra aurora
En mi horizonte grave como un ceño sombrío;
Revivirá en mis bosques tu gran risa sonora,
Que los cruzaba alegre como el cristal de un río.

Un día, al encontrarnos tristes en el camino,
Yo puse entre tus manos pálidas mi destino. . .
!Y nada de más grande jamás han de ofrecerte!

Mi alma es frente a tu alma como el mar frente al cielo:
!Pasarán entre ellas tal la sombra de un vuelo,
La Tormenta y el Tiempo y la Vida y la Muerte!

del libra *El libro blanco* (1907) de Delmira Agustini

---

[24]Quoted in, Gaston Figueira, "Daughters of the Muse," *The Americas*, Vol. 2, No. 11 (1950), p. 28.

From Far Away

In slow procession one by one,
*   silently*
I hear the hours pass,
*   rhythmical and cold . . .*
Ah! I always weep when you
*   are far away*
Smiling, even in sleep, when
*   your footsteps sound.*

I know you will return; another
*   dawn*
Darkly will frown over my dim
*   horizon.*
Your ringing laughter in this
*   wilderness*
Will echo like distant crystal
*   waters.*

The day we sadly met along
*   the road*
I placed my fate into your pale
*   white hands.*
Nothing greater had they to
*   offer you!*

My soul and yours facing each
*   other are*
Like sea and sky, between
*   them, like the shadow*
Of a flight, pass Storms and
*   Time, Life and Death.*

Delmira Agustini
translated by D. M. Pettinella[25]

For you, what is this poem
about? Does anything about it
seem to anticipate Delmira
Agustini's violent death? Why do
you think she is still considered a
major poet?

7. In an interview, Victoria Ocampo,
the Argentine writer, told of
having her first essays published
when she was 30 years old. She
described the reaction of her
parents to their publication. *"My*
parents were as afraid for me
of the road that I proposed to
follow, as they would have
been for a son—intent on
exploring a country of
cannibals."[26]

Why do you think her parents
were so afraid for her when she
first began publishing? Do you
think they had any legitimate
reason to be fearful?

[25]Quoted in, Agosin, "The Silent Voices," p. 25.

[26]Doris Meyer, *Victoria Ocampo, Against the Wind*
and The Tide (New York: George Braziller, 1979),
p. 45-46.

D. Women In The Military—Soldaderas In The Mexican Revolution

In the 7th century B.C., the Middle Eastern King Assurbanipal commemorated his military victories with a series of stone carvings. They show soldiers attacking on foot and horseback as well as a siege of the city of the Elamites (page 44). These carved battle scenes are very early examples of military themes used as subjects of works of art. Military subjects are common ones, from these of Assurbanipal to scenes that include George Washington, such as the painting by artist John Trumbull on page 45. But few of these historical art works include women subjects. Assurbanipal's siege scene hides from view the women in the city who supplied—and were part of—battlement defenders. The grand paintings of the United States Revolutionary War do not include the women who frequently worked as the quartermaster corps—and as soldiers—with these armies. But, historical records, diaries, travelers'

observations and even some remaining pay receipts tell us that women have had military roles. If women were mentioned in military history books, they were often put down as *"camp followers."* This term implied that women with armies merely trailed along as prostitutes.

Current historians are reevaluating women's military roles. They have found that women often provided the quartermaster and commissary duties that kept the armies going—finding food, preparing the meals as well as doing the washing and nursing. In times of war they carried water for cooling the artillery pieces and became involved in the fighting. Not only were women *with* the armies, but they were *in* some armies. Women in George Washington's army, for example, were assigned duties, paid, expected to fulfill their employment responsibilities and if they failed, were court-martialed. Historians have

43

Assurbanipal's Siege of the Elamites

just begun to research the ways various armies operated, but until modern times it is likely that most armies in history depended on the women who moved with them to do many indispensable duties.[1]

This was certainly the case with armies in Latin American history. Though the cultural ideal for women was that of the secluded woman, the reality of Latin American history was that many women joined—or were forced to join—the marches of armies. Until the middle of the 19th century, officers' wives often accompanied their husbands on campaigns. Lower-class women frequently went to war with their men mainly to do the cooking because making the staple food, corn tortillas, is a laborious task that requires special skill. Women often foraged

for food and did many other tasks. The following describes the ravañas, Peruvian women who were a part of the Peruvian army. The French-Peruvian writer, Flora Tristan, observed in the 1800's:

"In Peru, each soldier brings with him as many women as he wants: there are some who have as many as four. . . . The ravañas are armed; they load cooking pots, tents, all the baggage onto mules; they tow along after them a multitude of children of all ages, make their mules trot briskly, run

---

[1]See: Linda Grant Depauw "Women in Combat," *Armed Forces and Society*, Vol. 7, No. 2 (Winter 1981), Barton C. Hacker "Women and Military Institutions in Early Modern Europe: A Reconnaissance," *Signs* (Summer 1981), p. 643-671.

Washington's capture of the Hessians at Trenton, by John Trumbull

along behind them, and that way climb high mountains covered with snow and swim across rivers, carrying one and sometimes two children on their backs. When they get to the place that they have been assigned to, their first job is to choose the best spot for camping. . . . If they are located not far from an inhabited place, a detachment of them descends on it to get supplies, throwing themselves on the village like famished beasts and demanding provisions for the army from the inhabitants. When they're given them with good will, they do no harm, but if anyone resists them they fight like lionesses. . .plunder the village, bring the spoils back to camp and share it with everybody.

"These women, who provide for all the soldiers' needs, who wash and mend their clothes, receive no pay and have as their only salary

the right to steal with impunity. The ravañas are not married, they belong to no one and are for whoever wants them. They are creatures outside of everything; they live with the soldiers, eat with them. . .are exposed to the same dangers and endure far greater weariness. When the army is on the march, it is almost always on the courage, the intrepidity of these women, who precede them by four or five hours, that their subsistence depends. When one thinks that while leading this life of hard work and perils they still have the duties of motherhood to carry out, one is astonished that any of them can stand up to it. . . ."[2]

---

[2]Quoted in, Dominique Desanti, *A Woman in Revolt: The Biography of Flora Tristan* (New York: Crown Publishers, 1972), p. 85-86.

Another traveler to Peru inquired about the status of these women within the army and found that the ravañas drew rations but received no pay. He commented that:

"They [the women] are always enumerated [numbered] in the rosters of troops and in the reports of casualties which read: so many men and so many [ravañas] killed and wounded; for they share the soldier's death as well as his privations."[3]

Besides women who went with armies as ravañas (or as soldaderas, the Mexican term), in the wars for independence there were women like the Mexican Patriot Prisca Marquina de Ocampo who rode into battle with her saber drawn.[4] Most of the women who fought were part of their father's, brother's or husband's regiments, but some women dressed as men so they could fight as men. A British traveler in Brazil in the 19th century met Doña Maria de Jesus who fought in male uniform. She described their meeting:

"August 29th, 1823—To-day I received a visit from Doña Maria de Jesus, the young woman who has lately distinguished herself in the war of Reconcave [when Brazil declared its independence from Portugal]. Her dress is that of a soldier of one of the Emperor's battalions, with the addition of a tartan kilt, which she told me she had adopted from a picture representing a highlander, as the most feminine military dress. . . .

"The women of the interior spin and weave for their household, and they also embroider very beautifully. The young women learn the use of fire-arms, as their brothers do, either to shoot game or defend themselves from the wild Indians.

Doña Maria de Jesus

"Doña Maria told me several particulars concerning the country, and more concerning her own adventures. It appears that early in the late war of the Reconcave, emissaries had [traveled] the country in all directions, to raise patriot recruits; that one of these had arrived at her father's house one day about dinner time; that her father had invited him in, and that after their meal he began to talk on the subject of his visit. He represented the greatness and the riches of Brazil, and the happiness to which it might attain if independent. He set forth the long and oppressive tyranny of Portugal; and the

---

[3]William Eleroy Curtis, *The Capitals of Spanish America* (New York: Frederick A. Praeger, 1969), p. 348.

[4]Janet Kentner, The Socio-Political Role of Women in the Mexican Wars of Independence, 1810-1821," unpublished Ph.D. dissertation, Loyola University, 1975, p. 242.

meanness of submitting to be ruled by so poor and degraded a country. He talked long and eloquently of the services Don Pedro had rendered to Brazil; of his virtues, and those of the Empress: so that at the last, said the girl, "I felt my heart burning in my 'breast.'" Her father, however, had none of her enthusiasm of character. He is old, and said he neither could join the army himself, nor had he a son to send thither; and as to giving a slave for the ranks, what interest had a slave to fight for the independence of Brazil? He should wait in patience the result of the war, and be a peaceable subject to the winner. Doña Maria stole from home to the house of her own sister, who was married, and lived at a little distance. She [retold] the whole of the stranger's discourse, and said she wished she was a man, that she might join the patriots. 'Nay,' said the sister, 'if I had not a husband and children, for one half of what you say I would join the ranks for the Emperor.' This was enough. Maria received some clothes belonging to her sister's husband to equip her; and as her father was then about to go to Cachoeira to dispose of some cottons, she resolved to take the opportunity of riding after him, near enough for protection in case of accident on the road, and far enough off to escape detection. At length being in sight of Cachoeira, she stopped; and going off the road, equipped herself in male attire, and entered the town. This was on Friday. By Sunday she had managed matters so well, that she had entered the regiment of artillery, and had mounted guard.

She was too slight, however, for that service, and exchanged into the infantry, where she now is. She was sent hither, I believe, with despatches, and to be presented to the Emperor, who has given her an ensign's commission and the order of the cross, the decoration of which he himself fixed on her jacket.

"She is illiterate, but clever. Her understanding is quick, and her perceptions keen. I think, with education she might have been a remarkable person. She is not particularly masculine in her appearance, and her manners are gentle and cheerful. She has not contracted any thing coarse or vulgar in her camp life, and I believe that no [scandal] has ever been substantiated against her modesty. One thing is certain, that her sex never was known until her father applied to her commanding officer to seek her."[5]

In Costa Rica, Pancha Carrasco Jimenez fought in the war involving the United States adventurer William Walker. She acted as both nurse and cook but also fought as a soldier. Later she was decorated for bravery and given a general's full military honors at her funeral.[6]

Other women who went into war as soldiers, not soldaderas, were the Paraguayan women who fought in the desperate battle of Piribebuy in the Paraguayan War of 1864-70. With outdated weapons—and when finally reduced to stones and

[5]Maria Dundas Graham, *Journal of a Voyage to Brazil and Residence There During Part of Three Years, 1821, 1822, 1823* (New York: Frederick A. Praeger, 1969), p. 292-294.

[6]Arlene Schrade, Associate Professor, Secondary Education, University of Mississippi, unpublished paper.

sticks—they made one of the bravest, yet most "futile acts of defiance" in Latin American military history. Six hundred women died at Piribebuy.[7]

Whether in Paraguay, Peru, Colombia or Brazil, women were part of Latin American armies, but the women soldiers who became best known were the soldaderas of the Mexican Revolution of 1910.

The Mexican Revolution (1910-1917) has been difficult for historians to describe. This revolution began as a revolt against the Mexican government of Porfirio Diaz. Many Mexicans thought Diaz catered to wealthy investors and failed to make needed land and social reforms. The Revolution became more complicated when leaders such as Francisco Madero and Emiliano Zapata were killed. Women, as well as men, were caught between the various factions trying to take control. There were terrible incidents of Roman Catholic nuns raped and Native American women carried off to work in ammunition plants. For some people the Mexican Revolution seemed the beginning of a more democratic Mexico. For others, as one Mexican woman said, the Revolution was just a period of violence in which men were doing **"nothing more than going around stealing and violating girls."**[8]

One aspect of the Mexican Revolution that is not disputed is the participation of women soldaderas. Photographs provide clear evidence of their participation. Edith O'Shaughnessy, the wife of the American ambassador to Mexico, watched as press gangs gathered women together to do forced labor such as grinding corn and making

Young girl equipped with a rifle and ammunition—A soldadera in the Mexican army

tortillas for the army. Edith O'Shaughnessy described these Mexican women:

"A thick and heartbreaking book could be written upon the soldadera—the heroic woman who accompanies the army, carrying, in addition to her baby, any other mortal possession, such as a kettle, basket, goat, blanket, parrot, fruit, and the like. These women are the only visible commissariat for the soldiers; they accompany them in their marches;

[7]James D. Henderson and Linda Roddy Henderson, *Ten Notable Women of Latin America* (Chicago: Nelson-Hall, 1978), p. xv.

[8]Quoted in, Frederick Turner, *The Dynamic of Mexican Nationalism* (Chapel Hill: The University of North Carolina Press, 1968), p. 200.

they forage for them and they cook for them; they nurse them, bury them; they receive their money when it is paid. All this they do and keep up with the march of the army, besides rendering any other service the male may happen to require. . . . And they keep it up until, like poor beasts, they uncomplainingly drop in their tracks—to arise, I hope, to Heaven.''[9]

A British woman caught between the armies who escaped with the Federal troops had firsthand observations of the soldaderas:

''Mrs. Mestrezat and I treated ourselves to a full meal again. . . . The officers too were living well; and at this time the camp followers had no difficulty in securing food for the soldiers. In those days the Mexican army had no regular commissary department and the soldiers brought their 'women' with them to cook and care for them—women worn gaunt with hardship who could fight like she-devils if need be, and who were yet wonderfully gentle and compassionate to their men. While the men were fighting their way ahead, these women would slip through the lines and go on to the place where the army was to stop, and it was seldom that the soldiers failed to find something savory stewing or broiling over the charcoal when they arrived. On long marches the women carried the soldiers' money in order to buy the food; but the food was not always bought and paid for.

''I remember an officer telling me with great gusto how on one occasion, when our army was coming through the little village of
Chapultepec, not far from Cuernavaca, the soldaderas 'caught' their dinner, as they say. The improvised commissary squad of female foragers had arrived, as usual, ahead of the tired, hungry troops, and had spied at once flocks of fine fat turkeys, hens, and chickens. They had money, for the Federals were still being paid, and they offered to buy what they needed of this tempting poultry display. But the owners of the poultry were Zapatistas [followers of the Zapata faction]. They refused to sell to the Federals' women at any price. 'Que bueno!' (How nice), said the soldaderas. 'Then we shall take them! We must have food.' And with that, they chased the fowls and took the plumpest, while the owners stood by not daring to oppose them. Everybody knew the soldaderas!''[10]

Later on, when food became scarce and people began starving, her respect for the women grew:

''The wonderful soldiers' women—none like them in the world for patience and bravery at such times—combed the town for food, and when they could not get it any other way they stole, whatever and wherever they could, to nourish their men. These were the type of women who one day, in the north, when their men ran short of ammunition, tied their rebozos to the ammunition cart and hauled it to them. I bow in

---

[9]Edith O'Shaughnessy, *A Diplomat's Wife in Mexico* (New York: Harper Brothers, 1916), p. 144-145.

[10]Rosa King, *Tempest Over Mexico* (Boston: Little Brown & Co., 1936), p. 176-177.

respect to the Mexican woman of this class—the class despised by the women of indolent wealth, ignorantly proud of their uselessness. The Mexican women who marched with the Mexican soldier, who went before him to the camping place to have refreshment ready. Who nursed him when sick and comforted him when dying, were helpers and constructionists, doing their part in laying the foundation of this liberal government of today. Mexican women of education, just emerging from your shells of blindness, remember this and honor wherever she may be found, the Mexican soldier's woman!" [11]

Outsiders often found much to respect in these women, but what did the women themselves think about being soldaderas? An American journalist, John Reed, traveled with another Mexican leader's army, that of Pancho Villa. Reed tried to learn about the feelings of these women. He watched Elizabetta, a woman whose man had been killed, as she transferred her loyalty to another soldier, making his fire and husking his corn. She suddenly cried out, *"Oh, but this war is no game for women."* [12] Other women were more independent. One woman claimed that if she heard any more complaints from her man she would go off and join the opposing army. [13] Perhaps the majority felt like the women whose quiet conversation John Reed described:

"About two o'clock in the morning I came upon two soldaderas squatting around a fire, and asked them if they could give me tortillas and coffee. One was an old, gray-haired Indian woman with a perpetual grin, the other a slight girl not more than twenty years old, who was nursing a four-months baby at her breast. They were perched at the extreme tip of a flat-car, their fire built upon a pile of sand, as the train jolted and swayed along. Around them, backed against them, feet sticking out between them, was a great, inconglomerate mass of sleeping, snoring humans. The rest of the train was by this time dark; this was the only patch of light and warmth in the night. As I munched my tortilla and the old woman lifted a burning coal in her fingers to light her corn-husk cigarette, wondering where her Pablo's brigade was this night; and the girl nursed her child, crooning to it, her blue-enameled earrings twinkling,—we talked.

"'Ah! it is a life for us viejas' [travelers], said the girl. 'Adio, but we follow our men out in the campaign, and then do not know from hour to hour whether they live or die. I remember well when Filadelfo called to me one morning:...

"Come! we are going out to fight because the good Pancho Madero has been murdered this day!' We had only been loving each other eight months, too, and the first baby was not born....We had all believed that peace was in Mexico for good. Filadelfo saddled the burro, and we rode out

---

11*Ibid.*, p. 183.

12John Reed, *Insurgent Mexico* (New York: D. Appleton and Co., 1914), p. 105.

13*Ibid.*, p. 187.

Soldaderas marched with the Mexican Army

through the streets just as light was coming, and into the fields where the farmers were not yet at work. And I said: 'Why must I come?' And he answered: 'Shall I starve, then? Who shall make my tortillas for me but my woman?; It took us three months to get north, and I was sick and the baby was born in a desert just like this place, and died there because we could not get water. That was when [Pancho] Villa was going north after he had taken Torreon.''

"The old woman broke in: 'Yes, and all that is true. When we go so far and suffer so much for our men, we are cruelly treated by the stupid animals of Generals. I am from San Luis Potosi, and my man was in the artillery of the Federacion when Mercado came north. All the way to Chihuahua we traveled, the old fool of a

Mercado grumbling about transporting the viejas. And then he ordered his army to go north and attack Villa in Juarez, and he forbade the women to go. Is that the way you are going to do, desgraciado? I said to myself. And when he evacuated Chihuahua and ran away with my man to Ojinaga, I just stayed right in Chihuahua and got a man in the Maderista army when it came in. A nice handsome young fellow, too,—much better than Juan. I'm not a woman to stand being put upon. . .''

"I suddenly noticed that the light of our fire had paled, and looked up in amazement fo find it was dawn. Just then a man came running along the train from up front, shouting something unintelligible, while laughter and shouts burst out in his wake. The

sleepers raised their curious heads and wanted to know what was the matter. In a moment our inanimate car was alive. The man passed, still yelling something about 'padre,' his face exultant with some tremendous joke.

"'What is it?' I asked.

"'Oh!' cried the old woman. 'His woman on the car ahead has just had a baby!'"[14]

Though it was the soldaderas who often provided the commissary (the basic provisioning) for the army, women also served as officers. This was so much the case that one author claimed every troop seemed to have a *"famous lady colonel."*[15] Among these women were Rosa Mojica Bobadilla, Remedios Farrera, Amelia Robles and Maria de la Luz Espinosa Barrera. Colonel Barrera served with Zapata's army and was promoted for her bravery in battle. In an oral interview conducted in 1973, when she was 86, Colonel Barrera told how frightened she was at her first battle. She remembered the nervous jingling of her spurs before it began—but proved her bravery in battle again and again.[16]

How were women rewarded for fighting in the Revolution? Maria de la Luz Espinosa Barrera got a pension, eventually—but she was one of a very few who did. Little legislation for women's rights was passed after the Revolution; Mexican women were not allowed to vote in national elections until 1958. One observer felt *"the Revolution has done little purposefully, toward the emancipation of women."*[17] Another thought women's influence *"greatly increased"* through the Revolution, with more women becoming active in the professions and public life.[18] When Ana Maria Zapata, daughter of Emiliano

Zapata, gave speeches supporting women's rights, she often referred to the debt Mexico owed its soldaderas.[19]

In the 1930's the example of the brave and patriotic soldadera was used to further the cause of women's suffrage in Mexico. It has not, however, been used as an argument for allowing women to become professional soldiers, instead of temporary soldaderas. Most Latin American armies are now professional ones and women are not allowed to serve in these armies. There has been little agitation in Latin American countries to change this. Yet the masculinization of the military services denies women a career choice. Military service in some Latin American countries has been the avenue to political power and as a result, the exclusion of women from the military is another way of closing women off from the political process.[20] Women historically were an important part of

---

[14]*Ibid.*, p. 196-199.

[15]Anita Brenner, *The Wind That Swept Mexico* (New York: Harper Brothers 1943), p. 42.

[16]Anna Macias, *Against All Odds: The Feminist Movement in Mexico To 1940* (Westport: Greenwood Press, p. 42-43.

[17]Ernest Gruening, *Mexico and Its Heritage* (New York: Century Co., 1928), p. 627.

[18]Lillian Fisher, "The Influence of the Present Mexican Revolution Upon the Status of Women," *Hispanic American Historical Review* (February 1942), p. 211.

[19]*The Literary Digest*, "Mexican Feminists" (October 17, 1936), p. 12.

[20]It may also cause "macho" generals to make foolish decisions that a combination of male/female decision-making teams might avoid. If there had been women in the Argentine military they might have been better able to understand the decisions made by British Prime Minister, Margaret Thatcher and the British government in the Falkland/Malvinas Islands conflict than the Argentine generals.

Latin American armies. Currently Cuba alone admits women to officers' training school and its regular armed services. Guerrilla warfare in countries like Nicaragua and El Salvador have involved women as soldiers in modern times, but no formal or professional military services in Latin America admit women. The implications of women being barred from military service have yet to be explored—but at least one traditional occupation for women—soldadera—has been discouraged in modern times.

Points to Consider

1. Who were the ravañas? Why did Flora Tristan admire them?
2. How did Doña Maria de Jesus manage to serve in the Brazilian war of Reconcave? There is a long history of women who have used this method to serve in wars. What motives might they have had for going to such lengths to become soldiers?
3. How did the soldaderas help to feed the Mexican armies? Why might it be expected that they be able to fight as well as act as the quartermaster corps?
4. What are some of the specific hardships of the soldaderas that journalist John Reed described? What might make these women's lives even more difficult than those of male soldiers?

5. A cultural characteristic of Latin American societies has been the identification of men with *machismo* and women with *marianismo*. It would seem that women's participation in wars (either as officers or soldaderas) would oppose the cultural ideal for women which fits the marianismo model. Why do you think women frequently became officers in wars of independence and revolutions in Latin America? Why do you think male soldiers were willing to follow them?
6. Why do you think women do not serve in most present day Latin American armies?
7. From the stone carvings done of Assurbanipal to paintings commemorating George Washington's army, women are rarely seen in art with a military subject matter. Women have played crucial military roles throughout history—including that of Latin America. List reasons why you think they are not pictured, as are male participants.

E. The President's Wife Eva Perón and Tradition

Eva Perón was the wife of Juan Perón, president of Argentina from 1946-1955. But she was much more than a "First Lady" of Argentina. As one journalist put it, *"Eva held no official position but she ruled with Perón until 1952. In that year she died."*[1] In her autobiography, *My Mission in Life*, Eva described how she saw herself:

"I might have been a President's wife like the others. It is a simple and agreeable role: a holiday job, the task of receiving honors, of decking oneself out to go through the motions prescribed by social dictates. It is all very similar to what I was able to do previously, and I think more or less successfully, in the theater and in the cinema. . . .

"I was not born for that. On the contrary, there was always in my soul an open repugnance for that kind of acting.

"But also, I was not only the wife of the President of the Republic, I was also the wife of the Leader of the Argentines.

"I had to have a double personality to correspond with Perón's double personality. One, Eva Perón, wife of the President, whose work is simple and agreeable, a holiday job of receiving honors, of gala performances; the other, 'Evita,' wife of the Leader of a people who have placed all their faith in her, all their hope and all their love.

"A few days of the year I act the part of Eva Perón; and I think I do better each time in that part, for it seems to me to be neither difficult nor disagreeable.

"The immense majority of days I am, on the other hand, 'Evita,' a link stretched between the hopes

---

[1]V. S. Naipaul, *The Return of Eva Peron* (New York: Vintage Books, 1981), p. 102.

of the people and the fulfilling hands of Perón, Argentina's first woman Perónista—and this indeed is a difficult role for me, and one in which I am never quite satisfied with myself.

"There is no need for us to speak of Eva Peron.

"What she does appears too lavishly in the newspapers and reviews everywhere.

"On the other hand, it is interesting for us to talk about 'Evita;' not because I feel at all vain about being she, but because those who understand 'Evita' may find it easy afterward to understand her descamisados, [the destitute or, literally, the shirtless ones], the people themselves, who will never feel themselves more important than they are . . . and so will never turn into an oligarchy [rule by a few], which, in the eyes of a Peronista, is the worst thing that can happen."[2]

Her separation of herself between "Eva" (the wife of a man who was president) and "Evita" (the president's stand-in) illustrates a definition of the role of president's wife that went against traditional Argentine—even Latin American— views. There were women in Latin American history who had played significant roles as partners of political rulers. As mentioned earlier, in the 19th century Eliza Lynch had been an important influence on Francisco Lopez, dictator of Paraguay, perhaps preventing even worse abuses of power by him. Encarnacion Rosas was the wife of Juan Manuel de Rosas, dictator of Argentina in the mid-19th century. She strongly influenced her husband and seems to have run the country

Eva Perón—AP/Wide World Photos

Eva Perón as the glamorous wife of President Juan Perón

for two years while Juan Manuel was off fighting.[3] But by the 20th century, wives of Latin American presidents were expected to influence their husbands only behind the scenes. Carmen Diaz, the wife of the president of Mexico, was a pious woman whose public role was that of supporter of the Church. The wife of President Vargas of Brazil worked to aid social services. Some, like Julia Bustillos de Saavedra, wife of the president of Bolivia in the 1920's, supported the idea of women voting.[4] Presidents' wives, as a rule, were expected to be leaders of society, staying in the background, concealing any centralizing roles they played. In Argentina this

---

[2]Eva Peron, *My Mission in Life* (New York: Vantage Press, 1953), p. 60-61.

[3]Fleur Cowles, *Bloody Precedent* (New York: Random House, 1952), p. 39.

[4]Stella Burke May, *Men, Maidens and Mantillas* (New York: Century Company, 1923), p. 199.

genteel view of a correct president's wife was that she should be honorary president of charities, a dutiful homemaker and social organizer. This was what Eva Perón referred to when she said, *"I might have been a president's wife like the others."*

She was not like the others, as a brief review of her life story indicates.[5] Eva Perón was born in 1919 to Juana Ibarguren and Juan Duarte in a small rural town, Chivilcoy, Argentina. Her parents were not married but her father allowed her to take his name. She was, therefore, Maria Eva Duarte. After her father's death, Eva's mother ran a boarding house in s nearby town to support her five children. Eva left rural Argentina at 15 in the company of a famous singer who had come on a tour through their town. She moved to Buenos Aires to seek her fortune. There she worked as an actress in various theatrical productions and eventually in radio programs for which she was well paid. Some say her success was due to the men she met. It seems fateful that she did a series of radio programs on famous women of the world and their influence in history.

Eva Duarte met Juan Perón in 1943. Perón was a colonel in the cabinet and a man advancing within the military establishment. Eva moved into an apartment next to his and they began living together. Juan's wife had died several years before, and having a mistress was not considered unusual. Eva appeared with Juan at social occasions, however, and even at meetings, which was unusual. There was an uneasy feeling on the part of his fellow military officers that it was

not proper for him to be chasing after an actress so publicly. His sarcastic reply to criticism of his conduct was said to have been, *"Well, do you want me to chase actors?"* Their relationship continued but so did the resentment of Eva by Juan's military colleagues. There were various power struggles going on within the Argentine government in 1945. One faction arrested Perón and imprisoned him. The Perónist faction staged strikes and demonstrations, and Juan Perón was released. Historians have differed in their views of how large

---

[5]This article and the pros and cons of Eva Perón's career are based on:
Robert Alexander, *The Perón Era* (New York: Columbia University Press, 1951).
John Barnes, *Evita, First Lady* (New York: Grove Press, 1978).
Fleur Cowles, *Bloody Precedent* (New York: Random House, 1952).
Maria Flores, *The Woman With the Whip: Eva Perón* (New York: Doubleday, 1952).
Ruth and Leonard Greenup, *Revolution Before Breakfast* (Chapel Hill: University of North Carolina Press, 1947).
Nicholas Frazer and Marysa Navarro, *Eva Perón* (New York: W.W. Norton, 1980).
James Henderson and Linda Roddy Henderson, *Ten Notable Women of Latin America* (Chicago: Nelson-Hall, 1978).
Nancy Carol Hollander, "Women in the Political Economy of Argentina: unpublished Ph.D. dissertation, University of California, Los Angeles, 1974.
Mary Main, *Evita: The Woman With the Whip* (New York: Dodd & Mead & Co., 1980).
Paul Montgomery, *Eva, Evita* (New York: Pocket Books, 1979).
Marysa Navarro, "The Case of Eva Perón," *Signs*, Vol. 3, No. 1 (1977), p. 229-240.
Eva Peron, *My Mission in Life* (New York: Vantage, 1933).
J. M. Taylor, *Eva Perón: The Myths of a Woman* (Chicago: University of Chicago Press, 1979).
James Wilkie and Monica Menell-Kinberg, "Evita: From Elitelore to Folklore: *Journal of Latin American Lore*, Vol. 7, No. 1 (1981), p. 99-140. This article is good read in conjunction with the musical play "Evita" (Music by Andrew Lloyd Webber, Lyrics by Tim Rice) in discussing Perón's popular image.

was the part played by Eva in organizing the demonstrations, but it is clear that she was loyal to him. Shortly after his release they were married. After the wedding they went on an election campaign tour, working for Juan Perón's bid for the presidency. Perón became president of Argentina on June 4, 1946.

Eva Perón created her own part in his presidency. The old role of "President's Lady" was closed to her because as a poor, illegitimate country girl, actress and former mistress, she was not socially acceptable. The president's wife was traditionally asked to be president of *Sociedad de Beneficencia*, the largest charity group, run by women from wealthy, established families. The members used her youthfulness as an excuse to deny her the presidency. Eva offered her mother in her place, but the women of *Sociedad de Beneficencia* turned her down too. It was obvious that Eva, former actress and former mistress, was to be frozen out of any polite tasks done by a president's wife. After these slights, Eva developed a new role for the president's wife— that of "Evita," whose allegiance was to the poor instead of the rich. She had *Sociedad de Beneficencia* closed down and set up the *Eva Perón Foundation* in its place. All Argentine charitable activities went through her foundation. She had open hours at her office every day where the poor could come for help. She wore slacks in public, which no proper upper-class woman would have done. Eva Perón also supported women's rights issues such as divorce reform and women's suffrage. Further, she and her husband identified themselves with the *descamisados*—shirtless ones—

Eva Perón as "Evita"—leader of working-class Argentines whom she called "my people"

meaning people in shirt sleeves, not those in upper-class business suits. Her speeches and writings attacked the oligarchy—the ruling elite of what she termed ***"the rich, insensible to human sorrow."***[6] In rather high-handed ways, she and her followers forced contributions from large landowners and businesses to be given to the *Eva Perón Foundation.*

Even though she criticized the rich, Eva Perón took on the trappings of the wealthy. She said, ***"I live a reality which perhaps no woman has lived in the history of humanity."***[7] To put it more simply, one observer called her a ***"working girl made good."***[8] She wore lavish jewels and dresses, partly because she enjoyed them. She also wore

---

[6]Perón, *My Mission in Life*, p. 119.

[7]*Ibid.*, p. 65.

[8]Greenup, *Revolution Before Breakfast*, p. 166.

them to defy upper-class women of the oligarchy who considered jewels and clothes as their own status symbols. Eva Perón went on an elaborate tour of Europe called the Rainbow Tour. She was received by the Pope and European heads of state, which further enhanced her image. Although Eva Perón had real economic and political power—through her influence on Juan Perón and especially the *Eva Perón Foundation*, she had no official position within the government. She wanted to become vice-president of Argentina, but demonstrations organized in favor of her seeking the vice-presidency did not come off well. The army opposed her candidacy, and she eventually gave up the fight to run as vice-president. By the early 1950's it was discovered that Eva Perón was suffering from cancer, and she died in 1952.

Eva Perón's story does not end with her death. She was a controversial figure, deeply respected by many people of the lower classes but hated by many others—both by the wealthy and by those opposed to the political repression of the Perónist Era. Her body was preserved and plans were made to display it in a special memorial like that of the Soviet leader Lenin in Moscow. Plans were drawn up to have a huge statue built of her—larger than the Statue of Liberty in New York harbor. But Perón's government fell soon after her death. He eventually went to live in Spain. The embalmed body of Eva Perón was subject to a series of mishaps. First buried in Italy under an assumed name, it was then taken to Spain. There were demonstrations in Argentina for the return of Eva

Perón's remains and in 1976 she was placed in the Duarte tomb in a fashionable Buenos Aires cemetery. The tomb is constructed like a bank vault and protected with electronic sensors to alert the police if anyone comes too close.

Why all this controversy about Eva Perón's dead body? In the years following her death, Argentina has had a series of repressive governments and serious economic problems that made the Perónist Era seem a better time to many. Because of these problems, Juan Perón was recalled to govern Argentina in 1972 along with his third wife, Isabel. But Juan Perón died after two years. Isabel, who had been vice-president, became president of Argentina—the first woman president in the Americas. But though she tried to be another "Evita"—wearing similar hair styles to Eva and involving herself in charitable foundations—she did not have Eva's magnetism or believability as a leader. She broke down with mental exhaustion and her presidency was notable for both its repression and corruption. Perhaps what Isabel Perón's rule best illustrates is that she was not Eva Perón, there could be only one.

Most would agree that Eva Perón was a unique personality, but her role during the first Perónist Era is a highly controversial one. The following group exercise outlines arguments by historians and other observers regarding Eva Perón's career.

★　　★　　★

Group Exercise

After reading the above essay, in groups of four to six students, read over these opposing views of Eva Perón. Then assign a recorder and decide on the answers to the questions that follow.

Views Toward Eva Perón

Unsympathetic View

1. During the Perónist era, opposition leaders were arrested and exiled, newspapers shut down. Eva was seen as the **"woman with the whip."**

2. The Peróns led a lavish lifestyle, had many Swiss bank accounts and bankrupted the country. They used the Eva Perón Foundation for their own purposes.

3. Eva was an immoral woman who lived with a man to whom she was not married and whose improper behavior was an embarrassment to Argentina. She was considered a **"bad joke"** by some.

4. She attacked respectable women in fits of jealousy. When society women protested changes in the constitution, they were jailed as **"prostitutes."** One woman was denied burial in a church vault for **"health reasons."**

5. Eva used other women. She created a feminist organization that, then, gave no publicity to other feminists. She made the organization loyal only to Juan Perón.

6. Eva used charities only to try to gain political support for herself and Juan, with few long-lasting projects.

7. Eva's extravagance was self-indulgent, like the gold lamé dress she wore in Paris to attract attention. Some called her **"an overdressed hussy."**

8. Her writings are subservient to Juan Perón. To her, he is *"The Leader"* and she the humble little one. She preached unqualified loyalty to a dictator.

Sympathetic View

1. Governments before and after the Peróns illustrated similar disregard for civil rights—Eva Perón cannot be blamed for all the problems of Argentine politics.

2. Government corruption was not new to Argentina. The *Sociedad de Beneficencia* also had had a reputation as being partial to private interests.[9]

3. Argentine presidents were not criticized for their moral conduct or sex lives. Eva broke down the double standard and made virginity less a cult for women. She made possible a more honest discussion of sexual relationships.

4. Society women drew lines between themselves the other women, looking down upon lower-class women whose working lives were not considered proper. Eva showed more sympathy to lower-class women.

5. Women got the right to vote, divorce laws were changed to make them fairer to women, illegitimate children were recognized and university enrollments of women went up 139.51% during the Perónist Era.[10]

6. The Peróns recognized a real need for social services, especially those of hospitals, nursing homes and schools. Later regimes let their work go to waste but some social services continued.

7. Some poor people tended to take the attitude that, **"My wife can't have jewels, let Eva have them."** She became a symbol of what even a poor woman might become.

8. Although her speeches seemed to reflect her own ideas, she was politically dependent upon Juan Perón. She was, however, often a power behind his decisions and created a bond with the labor unions and Juan Perón.

---

[9]In a tour of Argentina in 1917-18, a British woman claimed that Sociedad de Beneficencia got "meager results" considering the amount of money collected. There were no records or financial statements made and there was more "patronage" than "humanitarian spirit." Katherine Dreier, *Five Months in the Argentine* (New York: Frederic Fairchild Sherman, 1920), p. 138-155.

[10]Hollander, *Women in the Political Economy of Argentina*, p. 281.

These opposing positions are not only limited to a textbook discussion. When "Evita," the musical play about her life, opened in London, there were boycotts and protests over the view presented in the play.[11] Those to the political left in Argentina (Socialists and Communists) have used Eva's image and her popularity with lower-class people to this day as part of their underground protest against the military right-wing government that ruled in Argentina until recently. Eva Peron's well-guarded tomb is still considered too controversial politically to allow the public to visit, and security force continues by her grave. Occasionally, despite the guard, someone slips in to light a candle in her honor.[12] The debate about her life continues, and for this Eva Peron would be pleased since she once said: ***"I confess that I have an ambition, one single, great ambition: I would like the name of 'Evita' to figure somewhere in the history of my country."***

Eva Peron, 1951[13]

★ ★ ★

Points to Consider

Deciding upon a response to a question or an issue is often a matter of judgment to which there may be no clear-cut answer. Historians judging the worth and impact of the life of a famous, influential person like Eva Perón are often confronted with the problem of weighing conflicting evidence. In the case of Eva Perón, the views in both lists—those sympathetic and unsympathetic—may be considered basically true. What makes one list sympathetic and the other unsympathetic depends upon the observer's point of view and any particular bias which the observer might hold.

---

[11]In an ironic footnote to history, the British troops departing to attack the Argentines in the Falkland/Malvinas Islands conflict in 1982, embarked on ships while the bands played, "Don't Cry For Me Argentina," the song Eva sings in the musical.

[12]Montgomery, *Eva, Evita*, p. 232.

[13]Quoted in Wilkie and Menell-Kinberg, "Evita: From Elitelore to Folklore," p. 99.

Deciding Your Group's Point of View

1. First decide as a group whether you are swayed by the sympathetic or unsympathetic view of either statement.
2. When you have decided on each of the eight statements, add up the columns of sympathetic and unsympathetic you decided on. (S and U)
3. Were a majority sympathetic? Unsympathetic? Or were you a combination of both?
4. If your group had a majority of unsympathetic, choose the two that seem the most powerful criticisms of Eva Perón. As a group, write a list of reasons for choosing those two criticisms. If your group had a majority of sympathetic—do the same for the above.

   If your group was a combination, pick one from each column and give reasons for choosing those factors.
5. Compare your answers in a class discussion. Why do you think that biographers and historians hold so many differing views of Eva Perón?

   Do you think that one view or another will eventually win out? Explain.
6. On October 30, 1983, Argentines elected their first civilian president in seven years. The Perónist candidate was Italo Luder—not Isabel Perón who was living in exile in Spain. The winner of the election was Raul Alfonsin of the Radical Civic Union (UCR) Party. Read the following newspaper article about Isabel Peron's return to Argentina in December, 1983.

Then answer the questions that follow.

Buenos Aires, Argentina

Former President Isabel Perón returned to Argentina Friday from two years of self-exile and accused the generals who ousted her in 1976 of trampling worker's rights and authorizing terror and the disappearance of thousands of citizens.

But she also praised Argentina's newest attempt at democracy and indicated she would seek control of the political movement that bears her name.

Perón, 52, returned to witness today's inauguration of Raul Alfonsin, Argentina's first civilian president in seven years. Several thousand Perónists welcomed her, chanting "Isabel! Isabel!"

The former president and widow of one-time strong man Juan Perón went to Spain in July 1981 after her release by the military regime, which had held her under house arrest for five years after her overthrow in March l976.

It was her position as the country's last constitutional president that brought her back at the invitation of Alfonsin to attend his inauguration.

In her arrival statement after a flight from Madrid, Perón thanked Alfonsin and pledged to cooperate with the new leader, even though he defeated the Perónist candidate in elections Oct. 30.

Her speech was mostly conciliatory, except toward the outgoing military government and the present Perónist leadership.

"Argentines," she said, "should congratulate ourselves for the portentous hour we are

living. . . . The people have recently imposed, once again, their unanimous will to travel the road of democracy.''

Still, she spoke of dangers and worries confronting the nation and said that she feels a responsibility "to contribute to the consolidation of the Perónist Party. . . and the necessity also to guide the action of the (movement) toward a harmonious relationship'' with other political groups.

Her role in the party has been a matter of mystery and concern by Perónists and non-Perónists alike since she left the country.

Most political leaders were afraid that her name alone could bring her back to power, although her administration was viewed as a disaster. Even many Perónist leaders privately disavowed her policies, or lack of them, during her time in office from her husband's death in 1974 until to her 1976 overthrow.

So when the campaign began for the recent elections, Perónist leaders excluded her followers and ignored Perón in spite of her title as party president, Perón, in turn stayed silent during the campaign and declined to even endorse the party ticket led by Italo Luder, who was once her attorney and president of the Senate during her time in office.

According to Perón's followers, who are known as ultra-verticalists for their belief that all power flows directly down from anyone named Perón, she now intends to get even.

Her attitude was shown in the arrangements for her return. She refused to deal with the party leaders and appointed a

welcoming committee to arrange her arrival that excluded all of themn. She also refused to meet with Luder and other party figures.

Perón plans to return to Madrid next week, supposedly to arrange her affairs and prepare for a permanent residence in Argentina and a restoration as the leader of Perónism.

★   ★   ★

From what you learned of Argentine politics, might there be a risk for President Alfonsin in allowing Isabel Perón's return? Explain. Why do you think Raul Alfonsin invited Isabel Perón to his inauguration? Why do you think the Perónist Party did not put up Isabel Perón as their candidate?

What do you think Isabel Perón might like to achieve in politics if she were to return permanently to Argentina?

After reviewing what you know of Argentina's modern political history, how would you judge the chances for Argentina to achieve a stable, democratic government? Briefly explain your answer.

Chapter 6

Women In Non-Latin America

A. Caribbean Women—An Alternative Ideal

The term Latin America is frequently used to describe areas of Central America, the West Indies and South America, in which Spanish, Portuguese or French are the primary languages spoken. These are Latin countries in the sense that their languages are based on the ancient language Latin, with many of their laws traced back to ancient Rome. Not all peoples in these areas are of Latin (Spanish, Portuguese or French) origin. Barbados, Jamaica, St. Kitts and the Cayman Islands were claimed and settled by people from Great Britain. The original peoples of the Caribbean area were Native American groups devastated by disease, war and enslavement by their European conquerors. A majority of the population of most Caribbean island countries are black people brought as slaves from Africa. The French in Martinique and St. Barthelemy; the Dutch in Aruba and Curaçao, as well as the British, controlled Caribbean islands where Africans were brought as slaves for plantation work. These slaves and settlers combined African and European cultures in Caribbean island settings to form cultures distinct from most of Latin America. Caribbean societies often have seen women with different roles than the ones generally accepted in Latin America. The following section deals with aspects of Caribbean women's lives representative of the differences.

Non-Latin Caribbean Women

Caribbean area countries are sometimes classified as an economically developing area because they have not exploited their natural resources and they lack an industrial base. Per capita income of the people in some cases is very low. Migration of adults to jobs elsewhere—to Britain, Canada, France or the United States—may be necessary to help support family members remaining on the islands. What this means for women, particularly working women, is that wage job opportunities may be scarce. The few available wage jobs, as well as government positions, usually go to men. Yet, particularly in the West Indies, education is highly valued for both sexes. The literacy rate in Barbados, for example, is 98%, one of the highest in the world.[1] As a result, a growing class of educated black women are becoming teachers, social workers, post office employees and doctors. These "new Caribbean women"[2] are often professional and political leaders, like Peggy Antrobus from Barbados, who is currently an undersecretary to the United Nations, and Eugenia Charles, named Prime Minister of the island country Dominica in 1983. These women act as role models for younger women and are sometimes referred to as "poor greats," that is, women who began poor but have achieved jobs with security and respect.[3]

Since professional job opportunities are limited in the Caribbean, women often support themselves in other ways. Becoming a domestic servant is one possibility. Light industry such as a small machine parts factory or garment work also provide some employment. Agricultural work on some islands in sugar cane or banana fields includes women. Some farm their own lands. Another way of earning money is through "higglering." "Higgerling" is a term applied to marketing women—the middle person between the farmer and the ultimate consumer—who collects goods from farmers, brings it to market and sells it.

Eugenia Charles, Prime Minister of Dominica

Women merchants, as in Jamaica, may be women who have regular farm routes for buying goods, who contract truck drivers, rent stalls at markets and have fairly substantial cash assets. Others are so-called "tray girls," poorer women carrying their entire stock of goods for sale, such as garlic or vegetables, on trays through the streets.[4] While

[1]Constance Sutton and Susan Makiesky-Barrow, "Social Inequality and Sexual Status in Barbados," in *Sexual Stratification*, Alice Schlegel, ed., (New York: Columbia University Press, 1977), p. 300.

[2]Gloria Joseph, "Caribbean Women: The Impact of Race, Sex and Class," in *Comparative Perspectives of Third World Women*, Beverly Lindsay, ed., (New York: Praeger, 1980), p. 158.

[3]Sutton and Makiesky-Barrow, "Social Inequality and Sexual Status in Barbados," p. 304.

[4]Margaret Fisher Katzin, "The Business of Higglering in Jamaica," *Social and Economic Studies*, Vol. 9 (1960), p. 298-300.

some of these women use public transportation to get to town markets, many walk for miles to sell their goods. This is particularly true for beginning higglers who have not built up routes with regular customers. The following describes one such woman:

"In late 1956, one young, inexperienced Riverside higgler began to buy flowers, but she had difficulty obtaining them because the farmers did not wish to antagonize the regular flower higglers who could be depended on to take all of their flowers throughout most of the year. However, she made the rounds of the growers every week, bought whatever flowers they were willing to sell to her and, to keep her expenses low, walked the 25 miles to Coronation with the flowers in a basket on her head. By May, 1957, she had been able to increase the size of her weekly load somewhat, but she was still walking to the market."[5]

Walking great distances and carrying large loads, particularly on hilly country roads, entails hard work. Yet, the women who do it often have a sense of pride in themselves because of the difficulties overcome in carrying on their family tradition of trading.[6]

One reason why employment of this kind is so important to women of the Caribbean is that many of the households are headed by females. The Caribbean family organization has been the object of much scholarly study and considerable controversy. The term "matrifocal" has sometimes been used to describe the common Caribbean family system in which most children are born outside formal marriage. A household is often made up of a

Haitian Higglers—FAO Photo

Haitian higglers travel to market by donkey

mother and her children, with a grandmother or sister lending additional support to the family. Not all Caribbean families fit this description. However, three different types of female/male relationships seem to form the most common life plan.

The first relationship is that of "visiting" or "friending." In this, the woman and man have sexual relations—and a child may result. But because of their youth, shortage of money or lack of seriousness, the woman continues to live at home and the couple does not marry. Ninety percent of the first children born to women on the island of St. Kitts, for example, are a part of

---

[5]*Ibid.*, p. 315.

[6]Joseph, "Caribbean Women," p. 153.

visiting relationships.[7] These visiting relationships may continue up to about age 25. But from ages 25-35, the second type of relationship called "living" is the more typical life-style.[8]

At this stage more children may be born into the family, causing heavier parental responsibilities; the couple lives together—but does not marry. Perhaps both the man and the woman are keeping their options open. They may not be able to afford elaborate wedding celebrations or to buy their own house, expected status symbols for those who marry.[9]

From ages 35-45, however, many people turn to the third type of relationship—marriage. One study conducted in Trinidad of the visiting-living-marriage life pattern found that approximately 60% of the men and women married, though not necessarily to previous partners.[10]

What these three types of relationships mean is that for the early years of most children's lives, they will live in households either headed by women or in households with "living" arrangements. Some outsiders saw these families as "denuded" (having no male household head) or "immoral" (when a relationship existed without marriage), and felt that the family arrangements were so unusual that they needed to be made more proper. Before independence, in Jamaica during the 1940's, the wife of the British governor, Lady Huggins, began a "Mass Marriage Campaign." Enlisting the help of churches, women's groups and government agencies, she tried to encourage people in living arrangements to be married. Her campaign had certain positive aspects for Jamaican women, such

as better economic protection for them and their children, but the campaign itself was a failure and petered out in 1955.[11] On the French island of Martinique, missionary groups came occasionally to give "beni peche" ceremonies—literally meaning "to make good a sin"—for couples already living together.[12] But outside of these occasions, family relationships on Martinique follow the same general Caribbean pattern.[13]

These marriage patterns—or the lack of marriage—have puzzled investigators. Often investigators feel that if a cause were found for these family patterns, perhaps the customs could be changed. But as reported by people in these cultures, there may not be a necessity for change. Here, briefly, are a few of the reasons investigators have given for

---

[7]Judith Gussler, "Adaptive Strategies and Social Networks of Women in St. Kitts," in *A World of Women*, Erika Bourguignon, ed., (New York: Praeger, 1980), p. 189.

[8]George Roberts and Sonja Sinclair, *Women in Jamaica* (Millwood: New York: Kto Press, 1978), p. 35-54.

[9]Judith Blake, *Family Structure in Jamaica* (New York: Free Press of Glencoe, 1961), p. 137-138.

[10] Patricia Voydanoff and Hyman Rodman, "Marital Careers in Trinidad," *Journal of Marriage and the Family*, Vol. 40, No. 1 (February, 1978), p. 159.

[11]Edith Clarke, *My Mother Who Fathered Me: A Study of the Family in Three Selected Communities in Jamaica* (London: George Allen & Unwin, 1966), p. iv-vii.

[12]Mariam Slater, *The Caribbean Family: Legitimacy in Martinique* (New York: St. Martins Press, 1977), p. 156-157.

[13]Yves Charbit, "Union Patterns and Family Structure in Guadeloupe and Martinique," *International Journal of the Sociology of the Family*, Vol. 10, No. 1 (January-June, 1980), p. 51.

Caribbean living patterns called matrifocal:

1. *Slavery* broke up the regular family structure among black slaves by often selling the fathers away from their families so that the mothers became the focus of the family.
2. An *African heritage* in which African women who were married to polygynous husbands (men who had more than one wife) often lived with their children in separate houses and were economically self-supporting, especially in West Africa, by doing trading.
3. A *Caribbean heritage* in which Carib Indians lived in separate female/male houses, with children living with their mothers.
4. *European models* such as British, Dutch and French white planters who took black women as concubines without marriage thereby setting an early pattern of non-marriage.
5. A *poverty culture*, which means that men who cannot find steady employment may leave women and children to survive as best they can. Landed people are more likely to marry because they have something to pass on to their children. West Indians who migrate to cities and strive to be like middle-class Europeans generally do marry.[14]

But whatever the causes for Caribbean marriage patterns, researchers have also found that they may fulfill the needs of these people. Men, especially those of uncertain financial means, may not want to take responsibility for supporting children. Placing the burden of such support upon women may seem unfair but women may actually prefer *visiting* or *living* to formal marriage. Legal marriage may bring more security but, as one woman said, *"**good** living **is better than bad marriage.**"* Or as another put it, *"**First you got to check a man out and get to know what you looking for.**"*[15] A survey of Jamaican women, whose unions with men were visiting ones, gave as their main reasons for preferring these relationships, that they afforded women freedom and independence, protected them from physical abuse and kept men from having control over female finances.[16] The sense that women must rely on themselves—and can do so—was reflected in the following quotation from a woman of the West Indies island of Montserrat:

*"**Women do run the households. West Indian men don't like to do any work at all either. A lot of West Indian men like to drink. Those that do work to support their families usually do not make enough to support their drinking habits and their families. So women have to go to work too. Some of them who have no education or who can't get jobs as domestics go out and plant a garden or do farming to make ends meet. Not only do these women work all day, but they come home and cook for their**

---

[14]Robert Bell, "Comparative Attitudes About Marital Sex and Negro Women in the United States, Great Britain and Trinidad," in *Women in the Family and the Economy*, George Kurian and Ratna Ghosh, eds., (Westport; Greenwood Press, 1981), p. 200.

[15]Quoted in Sutton and Makiesky-Barrow, "Social Inequality and Sexual Status in Barbados," p. 309-311.

[16]Roberts and Sinclair, *Women in Jamaica*, p. 67.

families too. They have to do it to keep the family going. Women are used to supporting themselves, so they do it when the men are here and when the men are gone as well. They tell their daughters not to depend on men, but on themselves. They should tell the sons to have responsibilities, but they don't. It is the women who become responsible.''[17]

This unflattering view of Caribbean men pictured above was not the case for all men. Many men not only supported their own families but also their sisters and even distant relatives. On the same island, one middle-class husband said:

"I take care of this old lady, she is not really related to me, but she was a good friend of my grandparents who raised me. I have known her for a long time. She has no one left to look after her, so I do. She must be about ninety years old now I guess. I take care of her because there is no one else to do it. I have an uncle who is a carpenter, he does a lot of odd jobs for me. I know that sometimes he doesn't do good work, but he is my uncle, and that's why I hire him.''[18]

Whether *visiting, friending, living* or *married*, many of the relationships between women and men in Caribbean societies are strong and deep. A British researcher in Jamaica recounted the following:

"It is firmly believed that the testing can be done only over a long period of living together. According to a Jamaican proverb, 'come see me and come live with me are two different things.'

"The period of free cohabitation, following as it may a number of experimental unions, is rationalized as a necessary trial of compatibility which is not only expedient but respectable, since it ensures the stability of the marriage which follows. Great contempt was often expressed for a couple 'who just picked up themselves and married right off.' One woman criticizing such a procedure said that if she herself were to get married she would have to live with the man about three years first. Married people must not only believe but know from experience that they can trust one another, and this was impossible 'if you just butt up a man one day and marry him tomorrow.' The result of these attitudes is that the ceremony is often postponed until after the birth of all or many of the children. One marriage in our records followed a concubinage of 14 years during which six children were born.

"During the trial period there are certain qualities for which the woman is 'tested.' Fidelity or the intention of being faithful is the first. A woman should show that she can be discreet and that she can justify the higher degree of confidence and trust which a wife has a right to expect. She should bear with poverty, if it comes their way, without discussing it with neighbors. She should not be familiar with anyone not her own equal. One man enumerated the qualities he looked for in a wife as speech, ability (in other words intelligence), and that she should have a good shape. He looked to see if she had

[17]Yolando Moses, "Female Status, the Family and Male Dominance in a West Indian Community," *Signs*, Vol. 3, No. 1 (Autumn 1977), p. 150.

[18]*Ibid.*, p. 146.

ambition and if she was familiar with anyone—man or woman—who was not 'qualified as herself.' (This he explained as meaning 'people who do not look up'.) She must be able to cook, too, and wash and do housework.

"Despite all this emphasis on practical qualities, it must not be assumed that, as one girl put it, 'love was not important.' We had a touching tribute by an old lady of ninety of her husband's devotion. He was her good husband she said, and excused her tears by explaining that when a man had been as good to you as he had been to her, you could not remember him without crying. He was faithful and a husband in need and deed. They were like 'kite and tail.'"[19]

There have been various family living styles especially among black people in the Caribbean. The acceptance in these groups of various sexual lifestyles have not, however, fit the middle and upper-class Latin American cultural ideal of the "locked away lady"—secluded and protected. The ideal Caribbean woman moved openly in society and was economically independent. This was not only true of black women, but was a cultural attitude that seems to have influenced white Caribbean women as well.

N. W. Manley (1893-1969) was a poor boy from Jamaica who became an outstanding athlete, Rhodes scholar, lawyer and Prime Minister of Jamaica. He recounted his background and his mother's role as family provider in his autobiography.

"My father was the illegitimate son of a woman of the people. . . .

"Mother was a woman of immense energy and vitality. She faced life with four children and no support except by her own efforts. The trip to America did not prove a success and shortly after her return [to Jamaica] she moved to Belmont [the family farm] where she lived with her children, a blind father, old Mr. Shearer, an invalid sister and yet another sister, a bright and lively woman who left for England a couple of years after.

"Mother had one great fixed determination in life: to see that her children, two boys and two girls, got a good education. Belmont was a hard place to manage. It was quite undeveloped, and like so many of the old derelict places in Jamaica, it carried on as best it could with a little of everything: logwood, sold after being cut into lengths of heart wood with bark and sap chipped off; a few cattle; a few tenants; a little cocoa. Single-handed she managed all these things and even found time to persuade the authorities to allow her to open a post office at Belmont, itself, which she took charge of. She made all our clothes; made jellies when guavas were in; kept a small chicken farm; and ran things with firm efficiency. When night came, she disappeared to her own room to write letters to her few remaining friends (nearly all of them deserted her when she married a near black man), and when not writing, was a wide and voracious reader.

"She was her own overseer and lived on friendly terms with the

---

[19]Clarke, My Mother Who Fathered Me, p. 83-84.

workers who respected her, and came with their personal troubles, but feared her temper which was high and indeed fearsome.''[20]

N. W. Manley's respect for his mother is part of the Caribbean and Latin American tradition that focuses on the importance of the mother in the family. His admiration of her as the supporter of the family represents a special characteristic of Caribbean women who were economically independent and heads of households.

★　　★　　★

Group Exercise

The following profile describes a typical farm woman on St. Lucia, a small island nation in the Caribbean. In groups of four to six, students should read over the profile and then, after appointing a recorder, answer the questions that follow:

Profile of Woman Farmer of St. Lucia

"The St. Lucian small-scale farm woman is in her middle-forties. She has one adult child living in the home with her and her husband/partner, in addition to one small grandchild and two school-age children. She was born in rural St. Lucia and lives in circumstances quite like those in which she was raised. She attended primary school for four years, and reads a little English, but speaks patois for everyday use. She is a 'married' [it may not a formal marriage] woman, and has close relationships with her own mother and others of her family. One of her children lives overseas and from time to time sends some money to aid the family.

"She and her family live in a small wooden house, some distance from the main road and accessible only by a 15-minute walk from the end of the bus route. The house is simple, but has water at a nearby standpipe, electricity, and a radio.

"The St. Lucian farm woman has had six children, one of whom she lost in its early infancy from a respiratory disease. Much of her everyday life revolves around the care and feeding of her children, including a year of breast feeding each one of them.

"Her work day is a long one. She rises very early, feeds her children and husband, then completes a portion of the work in her house before going to the field, frequently weeding for some 4 hours on their land, which lies a 30-minute walk away. She returns to the house in the late afternoon and begins the evening household work, dinner, and cleanup. On Friday she will often spend a half-day or more in the market at Castries, selling extra vegetables which have been harvested during the week. Her husband/partner will likely have taken charge of the harvesting and sale of bananas. An older child takes care of the grandchild and assists with the housework.

"Finances of the St. Lucian small-scale farm woman are a topic of great concern, for rising prices mean even food is hard to purchase in quantity and variety enough to be satisfactory. Almost 75 percent of total income is spent for food-stuffs. Clothing and

---

[20]Quoted in, Andrew Salkey, *Caribbean Essays* (London: Evans Brothers, 1975), p. 35-36.

school uniforms are also expense items, but necessary, for education of the children is highly valued by parents.

"Agricultural patterns employed on the farm have not changed much in her lifetime. In fact, she learned most of what she knows about farming from her own parents. Periodically she has had some farm animals, but currently has none. She does not know much about their husbandry. She participates with her husband/partner in many of the decisions made on the farm, but there are not really many decisions made, for in general they farm much as their parents did before them. Persistent problems for them are obtaining enough fertilizer and having means to transport their crops to the various marketing places, many of which are at a considerable distance from their home. She has had relatively little contact with the agricultural extension agent [from the university], though she knows he has been on the farm occasionally consulting on problems.

"The farm woman is much aware of the changing roles of women in contemporary society, and generally feels it means additional opportunities for women. She however, wants a traditional home and family for her daughter, possibly including a nursing career as well.

"The St. Lucian small-scale farm woman does not belong to any organizations except for her church. She, however, is aware of political events on the island, and knows her political representative well. She is somewhat skeptical about leadership in general and trusts mainly people she knows. Her principal contact with the larger world outside the immediate community is the radio.

"Her overall approach to life is a somewhat fatalistic one, as if control of her life were not very much in her own hands. Her principal personal desires revolve around maintenance of the family's way of life. On balance, she feels her life as a farm woman and mother has been a satisfying one."[21]

Reviewing the Profile

1. When the sociologist refers to a "profile," in this case she means an *average* woman—if you took all of the most typical characteristics, this description would fit.

   Jot down on a piece of paper:

   Number of individuals in the home

   Number of children

   Number of adults

   Total number

   Woman Farmer (describe in a few words):

   Education

   Family relations

   Work week

   Problems (describe two major ones):

   After reviewing this profile, discuss the following questions

---

[21]Barbara Knudson and Barbara Yates, MUCIA— *Women in Development Network* Interim Report of Research on "The Economic Role of Women in Small-Scale Agriculture in the Eastern Caribbean: St. Lucia," p. 97-98.

in your group and then write down your group's consensus (answers you collectively agree upon.)

2. How do you think this rural woman became aware of "changing roles for women in contemporary society?" How does she see her daughter's life, as the same or different from hers?

3. Describe her own family life and child-raising experience as to:
   • number of children
   • number of years of breast feeding
   • probable marriage pattern
   • focus of her emotional life

4. Why do you think this typical island woman:
   • is skeptical of political and other leaders
   • is fatalistic in her approach to life
   • "feels her life as a farm woman and mother has been a satisfying one"

5. Many recommendations to aid small farmers on St. Lucia and other Caribbean islands were made because of this study. The following are just a few of them. For each of these recommendations give:
   • a clue from the profile description that indicated the existence of the problem that each recommendation was meant to help solve.
   • a brief explanation of the way the recommendation might help to solve one of these farmers' problems.

Recommendations:

Programs meant to aid small-scale farmers should be aimed at the family or household, not the male farmer exclusively.

* * *

Extension personnel (university trained agriculture specialists) who give advice to farmers should be sensitive to the economic and social roles of small-scale farm women.

* * *

The media should be used more extensively to give farm information.

* * *

Expansion and diversification of small animal husbandry should be encouraged.

* * *

Women should be assisted in forming groups and organizations for mutual support and as a way to gain farming information.

* * *

6. Professor Barbara Knudson, one of the researchers who conducted this study, has commented that care must be taken before recommendations are made for "income generating" projects. These are projects—such as encouraging handicrafts or the production of additional farm products for market—that are meant to help increase family income. Frequently women are the ones who are encouraged to do income generating projects. What specific evidence is there that these women already have considerable work burden? Why might recommending income generating projects add to a woman's burden rather than help her to increase her income?

7. Looking back over both the article and the profile, why do you think outsiders have sometimes wanted to change family arrangements in the Caribbean? Why do you think these women seem comfortable with traditional families for their daughters—perhaps with some changes?

B. Native American Women In The Twentieth Century

Other Non-Latins in Central and South America to offer a variety of different customs for women are the various indigenous groups. Although many of these people have been absorbed into the Latin majority culture, especially isolated groups have managed to maintain their unique lifestyles and customs.

To many outsiders, the women of Latin American indigenous groups all appeared to fit one image, that of poor, long-suffering, hard-working, strong, yet silent women. The Chilean poet Gabriela Mistral wrote of a woman and man she saw:

"They might have been a joyous race; God put them in a garden, like the first couple. But four hundred years of slavery have dulled for them the very glory of their sun and their fruits; it has made the clay of their roads hard beneath their feet, yet it is as soft as fruit pulp.

"And this woman, whom the poets have never sung, with her Asiatic silhouette, must be like Ruth the Moabitess who labored so well and whose cheek, bent over the sheaves, was bronzed by the sun of a thousand afternoons."[1]

Not only poets, but many anthropologists researching Native American women in Central and South America, document these women as hard working. Anthropologists also make us aware that a single image of Native American women is really a stereotype. Studies suggest that there are considerable differences in the ways in which women spend their lives in the hundreds of indigenous groups and subgroups of

---

[1]Gabriela Mistral, "The Valley of Mexico: Silhouette of the Mexican Indian Women" in *Green Continents*, Germán Arciniegas, ed., (New York: Knopf, 1944), p. 79.

Ayamara women of Peru

Central and South America and the West Indies.

Attempting to classify the status and role of women in these many groups is difficult because anthropologists continue to investigate. Until the recent emphasis on women's history, some of these women's roles simply were not seen by researchers who tended to ignore women's activities as unimportant. Some groups may change their view of proper women's roles. In a study of the Mapuche of Peru carried out in 1964, a social scientist found that women were barred from the council of elders and that religious leaders were male;[2] yet historical investigations have now shown that the 19th century Mapuche had a tradition of a female *huepufe, "the public orator who spoke at great tribal ceremonies and who, because of the wisdom*

she manifested, was permitted to give her opinions publicly."[3] It is difficult to tell whether this custom died out or if the researcher in the 1960's was unaware of the female *huepufe*. There is still a great deal of necessary research to be done on indigenous groups of the past and present. But perhaps a look at three representative types of indigenous cultures will suggest the diversity present among the many groups of Central and South America. These three categories are those with:

- relative equality between the sexes
- responsible patriarchy
- extreme patriarchy

Relative Equality Between the Sexes

One group in South America whose culture favors equal relationships between the sexes is the Bari of the wilderness areas of Colombia. Beginning in 1964 a homestead movement encroached upon their territory. The Bari population dropped from about 1800 in the early 1960's, to 800 people a few years later.[4] The Bari are forest horticulturalists, planting crops and moving on to another forest area when the soil wears out. They have sexual divisions of some work tasks. Men weave the hammocks while

[2]Louis Faron, *Hawks of the Son: Mapuche Morality and Its Ritual Attributes* (Pittsburgh: Pittsburgh University Press, 1964), p. 186-187.

[3]Ximena Bunster, "The Emergence of a Mapuche Leader: Chile," in *Sex and Class in Latin America*, June Nash and Helen Icken Safa, eds., (New York: Praeger, 1976), p. 317.

[4]Elisa Buenaventura-Posso and Susan Brown, "Forced Transition from Egalitarianism to Male Dominance: The Bari of Colombia," in *Women and Colonization*, Mona Etienne and Eleanor Leacock, eds., (New York: Praeger, 1980), p. 113.

women gather and spin the sisal, the material for the hammocks. Many chores are crossover ones; both sexes are involved in fishing and house construction chores. If women are working in the fields, men may take care of the children. There are female as well as male healers, and singing is led by both sexes. This sense of communal life is described by a French investigator:

"At no moment of life do men affirm themselves as a group in opposition to women. On the rare occasions in which men get together without women (collecting the reeds for making arrow shafts, an important hunting trip) their getting together never appears as a collective activity, but rather is only a momentary association of independent individuals, all of whom are working for themselves and their families."[5]

The pattern of the Bari, of both sexes working comfortably together, is not followed by the Mundurucú of Brazil, but nevertheless an equality between the sexes is present in their society. The Mundurucú have a segregated society in which adult males sleep in the men's house and females live in houses with female relatives. The group is matrilocal, meaning a man who marries moves to the woman's village. Because women remain in their own villages, mother/daughter/sister ties are lasting ones. Researchers Yolanda and Robert Murphy found that:

"Among the Mundurucú, both men and women agree that the truly enduring bond is between mother and daughter, and this is how they phrase their matrilocal preferences: 'Mothers don't want to lose their daughters'; or 'How would a girl manage without her mother to help her?' The tie is indeed close. Mothers and daughters work together, they relax in each other's company, they are seemingly inseparable. This same unity carried over to the relations between sisters, who are expected to form enduring residential groups. Sisters must be loyal to one another, they must share, they are a unit. One of the two cases of suicide that we heard of among the Mundurucú was of a woman who lived in an extended family centered on three sisters. The people are very reluctant to talk about suicide, looking upon it as the worst of all crimes, a lethal blow to society itself, and we were not able to gather much detail beyond the simple statement that 'her sisters began talking about her.' This is classic phraseology among the Mundurucú for being frozen out, isolated, and either ignored or gossiped against, and it was clear that the woman preferred death to continued estrangement from her sisters. If the same thing happened among brothers, the disaffected one would simply have moved.

"The solidarity of the mother-daughter and sister-sister [ties] extends itself in diminished degree to a union of all the women of a household and, ultimately, of the village."[6]

Female ties, then, may be more important to women than the fact that Mundurucú men appear to do less work and have more political and religious ceremonies than

---

[5]Solange Pintor, quoted in, *Ibid.*, p. 119.

[6]Yolanda Murphy and Robert Murphy, *Women of the Forest* (New York: Columbia University Press, 1974), p. 122-123.

women. Divorce is common, with either sex able to end a marriage. The Murphys tried to find out who the Mundurucú saw as the "person in charge" in their society. There often seemed to be conflicts in opinions between men and women as to who was "in charge."

"In the early part of our field research, we were confused by the term wat, which we believed for a time to be roughly translatable as 'owner.' A person would be described to us as the owner of a house or of a garden, but it quickly became apparent that when we asked a man who was the 'owner' we would be answered with a man's name; when we asked a woman, we would be told that the owner was a woman. As we became more familiar with the language, we heard the same word applied to the ownership of a village, describing the function of the chief, or of a timbó fishing trip, or of a ritual. The word, it appeared, did not mean 'owner,' but 'person in charge,' or the one who took an initiative in some undertaking. When applied to houses and gardens, the different responses that we received from men and women also indicated a basic difference of opinion as to who indeed was in charge."[7]

The Mundurucú, then, may differ from the Bari in the segregated living quarters and tasks divided by sex, but women in both societies see their roles as equal to those of men.

Responsible Patriarchy

The term "responsible patriarchy" is one used by Eileen Maynard to describe differences she observed in Guatemala between the Pokomams, an indigenous group, and the majority group—the Ladino or Latin American society.[8] Both groups saw the male as head of the household and the proper family as patriarchal. Ladino men sometimes abandoned their wives and took pride in outside sexual conquests. The Pokomams men were most proud of their ability to perform hard work, to care for their family and to sustain family loyalty.

Pokomams women have a sense of security in their sex-segregated, patriarchal societies. Although both sexes do agricultural work, field work is primarily the man's responsibility. Men work long hours at hard physical work in the hot sun. Women are in charge of housekeeping and marketing of goods. This also entails much work. Other customs are less advantageous for women. Adultery by Pokomams men is overlooked while women are expected to be faithful to their husbands. A husband, however, is not supposed to desert or divorce his wife. As one Pokomams leader said, *"To leave my wife for another woman? Never."*[9] Men do have control of religious and political affairs in their community, but there is a sense that both partners are contributing to the economic success of the family. These women do not have many choices beyond their assigned roles. Education is discouraged for Pokomams women, and there is little chance for a woman to do anything out of the ordinary with her life.

---

[7]*Ibid.*, p. 68.

[8]Eileen Maynard, "Guatemalan Women: Life Under Two Types of Patriarchy," in *Many Sisters*, Carolyn Matthiasson, ed., (New York: Free Press, 1974), p. 95.

[9]*Ibid.*, p. 86.

Pisac woman, Peru

The Highland Maya of the Yucatan have a similar culture. Some women in the Mayan village of Chan Kom, studied by the anthropologist Mary Elmendorf, said that they looked forward to learning. One woman, refused an education as a child said, *"I just never had the chance to learn. . . . Now that we have women teachers, maybe they will teach me—I am going to ask them."*[10] Like the Pokomams, men's and women's roles in the Maya Highlands are sex segregated, men working in the fields and women in the household. The more restrictive tasks of household duties make some women look forward to going to the woods to get firewood. Even though the bundles are heavy, women seem to feel *"free in the woods"* as they cannot be at home.[11] At home the male of the household is in control. The men are

the first to eat, while women wait on them. The father controls family marriages, and choices are sometimes forced on the children. Physical punishment is sometimes used against wives and, although people appear to care for one another, Mary Elmendorf said, *"I never saw a husband and wife touching or even looking at one another affectionately."*[12] Divorce among the people of Chan Kom is rare.

Sexes are segregated from one another in work tasks, and men are dominant. There is respect for each other's economic contributions. When trying to find which sex thought it worked harder, a survey showed that:

"Men think women's work is harder and women say that men's work is harder. One element involved in this apparent contradiction seems to be that men perceive women's work as being confining, limited to the house and yard, while theirs is free of that constricting element. Women see men's work as being harsh, physically exhausting and therefore not as free as is theirs, since men do not have the opportunity to take advantage of free moments in the hammock, in the coolness of the home."[13]

It is perhaps this sense of mutual respect and contribution to the family welfare that makes Mayan women feel part of their community, even if leadership roles most often, though

---

[10]Mary Elmendorf, *Nine Mayan Women* (New York: John Wiley, 1976), p. 53.

[11]*Ibid.*, p. 28-29.

[12]*Ibid.*, p. 35.

[13]*Ibid.*, p. 104.

not exclusively, go to males.

Extreme Patriarchy

The term "repressive patriarchy" could best be used to describe the sort of society that uses the labor of women without offering much recognition or reward. The Yanomama of Venezuela seem to be one of these groups. Ceremonies and religious observations are directed by men. Men meet in the center of the village each night to talk loudly, while women sit quietly on the edge of the group.[14] Among the Yanomama, male kinship ties are considered the most important. "Brother-in-law" is a term of major respect. The title for kinship relationships among men, like brothers, fathers, fathers-in-law are considered to be much more important than sisters, mothers-in-law and mothers. Women marry outside their own villages, so their natal kinship ties are weakened by distance. Males—brothers and fathers—determine women's marriages, while husbands direct and control the rest of their lives.

Women are conditioned to be *"fearful and submissive."*[15] The staple food of the Yanomama is plantain (a kind of banana) that grows relatively easily. Although both sexes do agricultural work, males do not expend as much time growing crops as females. Men spend time in warlike preparations. Men also hold elaborate feasts when guests visit. Hallucinogenic drugs are used, and before long, loud dialogues between men are carried on.[16]

Finally, Yanomama women have not organized a mutual support system commonly found among women living in sexually segregated societies. For example:

"Meal preparation is carried out by each woman in her own section of the house. Even when co-wives are cooking simultaneously for the same husband, each will prepare the food that she herself has gathered or harvested. Two or more women may go out together to harvest garden crops, to collect wild foods, or to cut firewood, but once out, each woman goes about her own business. If they go in a group, this is in part because women avoid being alone at any distance from the house."[17]

Unfriendly relations between Yanomama men and women seem to carry over into the women's relationship to one another. The extreme patriarchal organization of this group appears to keep Yanomama women isolated and lonely as well as submissive.

Within the many different indigenous groups of Central and South America, women's status can differ greatly. Even groups sharing the same geographic area or the same basic economic conditions may have different cultural expectations for women. The status of these women may also be in considerable contrast to those of other Latin American women. A woman from the United States lived for a time with the Arawak of British Guiana (now Guyana) in the 1940's.

---

[14]Judith Shapiro, "Sexual Hierarchy Among the Yanomama," in *Sex and Class in Latin America*, June Nash and Helen Icken Safa, eds., (New York: Praeger, 1976), p. 98.

[15]Orna Johnson and Allen Johnson, "Male/Female Relations and the Organization of Work in a Machiguenga Community," *American Ethnologist* (Vol. 2, No. 4 (November 1975), p. 646.

[16]Shapiro, "Sexual Hierarchy Among the Yanomama," p. 97.

[17]*Ibid.*, p. 90-91.

Her description of one Arawak woman, Mano Sue, suggests a world that gave women quite a different sense of self than the Latin American ideal of a secluded, household-bound woman:

"Mano Sue's knowledge of jungle lore was superior to anything I had ever dreamed a primitive person could possess, and her knowledge of the heavens, moon and stars, was equally amazing. In childhood, she told me, she had learned about the celestial bodies from her parents and older Indians of her tribe. To this knowledge, in later years, she had added her personal observations. For nights in succession she would sit up all night alone to study the stars and moon as they moved slowly across the sky, from sunset to sunrise. She would keep track of any star that vanished overnight, not to return for weeks or months, or sometimes not at all. When a star disappeared, she said, she watched eagerly for its return night after night. While watching the stars, her ears were always attuned to the earthly noises—the gurgling of river water, the howl of some roaming night creature, or even the simple croaking of a frog or noise of an insect. Everything in nature had meaning to her. Everything had its rightful place in the universe she knew. She spoke of moon, stars, and sun as her sisters and brothers. Over and above these visible things, Mano Sue acknowledged a Greater Being. Simply and naively she believed in Him with all her heart. Papi was the Great Being's name, and it was He who had placed everything the Indians needed in the jungle for their use.

"I shall ever be grateful to Mano Sue for inviting me to join her on one of her nocturnal watches. During this night I learned more of what civilized people call 'astronomy' than I could ever learn, perhaps, from books. For my teacher was one who loved sun, moon, and stars as she loved insects, birds, and flowers. She thought of the entire Universe and all its contents as a whole, and she was a part of the whole, and the whole a part of her—all akin....

"At intervals during the night, I checked the time by my watch when the noises made by night creatures changed. It would be easy for a person to rely wholly on moon, stars, and insect noises for the hours if not the minutes. About four o'clock Mano Sue called my attention to the cricket's 'going-back-to-their-hole noise,' which I immediately realized was a distinctly different noise from the one they made when they started their twilight chirping.

"From that time until daybreak, Mano Sue and I said very little. We sat quietly watching and listening to the sounds that told us that some crawling or flying creatures were returning to their beds or others awakening to another day. Before dawn, birds began to stir in their nests and soon awakened, flying out to gather food for their young. A rabbit or labba scurried through the bush near by. The eastern sky took on a rosy hue, making ready for the coming of the morning sunrise. Soon it was daybreak."[18]

---

[18]Jo Besse McElveen Waldeck, *Jungle Journey* (New York: Viking Press, 1946), p. 210-212.

"genocidal" policies of Chile, Bolivia, Guatemala and Brazil that pushed indigenous peoples off their land and allowed their massacre without government intervention.[19] Groups like the Bari are becoming more "Latinized"—in other words, losing their system of equality between the sexes.[20] Native American cultures have maintained themselves throughout the four centuries of political domination by Europeans. It is not clear how much longer they will be able to hold on to their special ways of life.

★   ★   ★

Points to Consider

1. One way to classify societies—in this case indigenous groups—might be to place them on a continuum that shows who is "in charge." Such a continuum is:

2. There may be many reasons why societies vary so widely as to who is "in charge"—men, women or both. In studying comparatively small groups, like South snd Central American indigenous peoples, anthropologists have given different explanations for these differences. Anthropologists Orna and Allen Johnson explain the differences by the way work is organized. Another social scientist, Judith Shapiro, says that women's religious ritual roles and ceremonial activities may be crucial in explaining differences. What might be other possible reasons for these differences? Which answers,

Equity	*Responsible Patriarchy*	*Extreme Patriarchy*
Decisions are made together and consider the needs of both sexes.	Men make most decisions but keep in mind women's needs.	Women have virtually no say in running the society or deciding their own lives.

1	2	3	4	5	6	7	8	9	10

Using the information given in this article, place the following groups on the continuum:
Bari
Mundurucú
Highland Maya
Yanomama
Arawak

Now go back to earlier articles in the book and find six other groups mentioned (e.g., early pre-Columbian groups, upper, middle, or lower-class Latins, etc.). Place each (as you see it) on the continuum and give two brief reasons or pieces of

evidence for your classification. (Note that they can be placed from 1-10, so you might place a group between categories.)

including those of the anthropologists, do you feel best explain these differences?

[19]International Work Group for Indigenous Affairs, *IWGIA Newsletter*, March 1981, p. 82-83.

[20]Buenaventura-Posso and Brown, "Forced Transition from Egalitarianism to Male Dominance," p. 123-131.

C. Black Caribs Of Belize—A Special Religious Role For Women

Group Exercise

The Black Caribs represent an unusual non-Latin group in northern South America. These people have kept their own values and customs that differ from both the groups of indigenous peoples studied and the dominant Latin culture. These values include a special role for older women in the religious life of the community.

The Black Carib are people of African and Native American descent. They live in over 50 settlements along the coast of the Caribbean Sea and speak Carib, a Native American language. The Black Caribs described here live in a community in the small country of Belize. Virginia Kerns, an anthropologist from the United States, lived among a a Black Carib community in the mid-1970's. She was especially interested in Black Carib death rites and the prominence of older women in these rituals. Her description of a few of these rites follows. In groups of four to six students, read over her description and, after appointing a recorder, answer the questions that follow.

Background

"Today gardening provides relatively little food or income [for the Black Caribs]. Some men work at nearby plantations and return home to their families on a frequent and regular basis. Many other men and young women work as unskilled laborers all over the country, coming home only occasionally. Most of the older people who live in Black Carib villages are men and women who cannot find work, either because of physical disability or in the case of women, because of age discrimination in the labor market. . . .After the age of forty or fifty a Black Carib woman finds it very difficult to obtain any regular employment aside from the lowest

Late 19th century photograph of Black Carib women grating cassava

paying kinds of domestic work. Most older women must depend on others for support—either their grown children or, if they are married, their husbands.

"While marital relationships are relatively unstable, the Black Carib consider the parent/child bond to be perpetual, one that even death cannot sever. . . like her mother before her, the older woman increasingly depends on her daughters and sons for support. And while there is no law that compels their support, morality demands it, and women do their best to encourage it. For the Black Carib, a moral person is a generous and responsible one who honors the obligation to 'help' kin, in whatever manner necessary. An immoral person is a stingy and negligent one. As young mothers, women instill the traditional values of generosity and sharing in their children; from a very tender age a child's refusal to share

brings swift punishment.

"Although these Black Caribs in Belize are practicing Roman Catholics who insist their children are baptized, villagers believe that many different spirits, both human and non-human spirits are entirely hostile to the living, while the spirits of lineal kin can either protect or harm their living descendants. . . If the living neglect their dead kin, they can expect to suffer for it. Their ancestors may cause them to sicken and even die, and the only protection against such misfortune, and the only cure for it, is careful attention to the needs and demands of the dead. . . ."

Mourning

"The needs of the dead are met through public ceremony. . . The sound of women wailing is the first public signal of a death in any Black Carib village. Kinswomen of the deceased begin their customary

Black Carib women baking wheat bread

display of grief as soon as they hear of the death... While a few elderly women work in private preparing the corpse for burial, several men hastily construct a coffin. When the wake begins after dark, the coffin is finished and has been placed in the main room of the house. Men, women and children go there to view the body, and many of the adults linger to express their 'appreciation' of the deceased... The next day people gather briefly in the church to pray. Then a procession of women, children and a few men follows the male pallbearers and coffin to the burial ground. As the men lower the coffin into the grave, kinswomen of the deceased begin to wail again....

"Death, like sickness, is not a matter for private suffering, borne alone or in silence. Death draws the living together... Close kinswomen of the deceased begin to wail, in a customary display of grief, as soon

as they hear of the death. Preparations for the wake proceed almost immediately, and primarily involve women, both close relatives of the deceased and other women who volunteer their help to them.''

Visitation and Wake

"A number of tasks must be accomplished before burial the next day. The body of the dead woman or man must be washed and dressed for burial, usually by old women...

"While a few men work in the yard, constructing a wooden coffin, women begin to prepare refreshments in the kitchen and over open fires in the yard. On short notice they need to assemble a sufficient amount of coconuts, flour, and other ingredients to make bread, and rice or corn to be roasted and then boiled for gafe, a black coffee-like drink that they sweeten heavily with sugar. The women will distribute this food throughout the night to kin and friends of the deceased who attend the wake.

"Wakes are sedate affairs early in the night. The men gamble or converse, a few women sing hymns, and others sit together talking quietly or help distribute food and rum. In proportion to the amount of rum passed around, conversation grows more animated and the crowd more convivial [friendly] in the night. Eventually someone induces a few of the men to provide music for dancing, substituting wooden crates for drums, the usual and preferred instrument. Some of the older women are sure to protest the impropriety of festive music and dance, but only halfheartedly and usually in vain. Soon enough they may take a turn dancing themselves.

"Throughout the night and the next morning, before the burial, some relatives of the deceased— especially close kin, and usually more women than men—arrive from other communities. As the women arrive, each begins to wail. Wailing is song-like and starkly beautiful, a highly stylized but very moving expression of sorrow. When a woman wails she expresses her gratitude for the support and care that person gave her. She speaks tearfully and at length, always in Carib, about the virtues of the dead man or woman. If she is skillful, she will move some of her listeners to tears as she reminisces about the deceased and mourns her loss.

"Wailing is a ritual skill that women cultivate, and some women were thought to wail especially well. People criticize a woman who cries quietly or spiritlessly, calling her ungrateful. Men rarely wail. They customarily approach the open coffin and address a few words of appreciation and farewell to the deceased, speaking stolidly if somewhat tearfully."

Burial

"There are other moments when the bitter finality of death also grips survivors. . . The widow, sisters, and daughters of the deceased, who contain their grief in church and while they walk in the funeral procession to the burial ground, customarily abandon themselves to displays of intense sorrow at graveside. Other men and women must physically support them, helping them away from the burial site after the prayers end."

Ninth-Night Wake-After Burial

"Black Caribs explain that the ninth-night wake is a kind of farewell party for the dead man or woman, who 'resurrects' on the third day after burial and then wanders about aimlessly, 'bothering' the living— unless given a proper send-off to the next world. . . . The women also distribute rum throughout the night. After the prayers at dawn, they abruptly tear down the novena altar, while kinswomen of the deceased wail briefly one final time. This marks the end of the ninth-night wake."

Conclusion

"Older women figure in [all] of Black Carib death rites in a number of important ways. They organize and provide most of the necessary labor and expertise for the events, and they represent their kin in certain ceremonies. In many ceremonies they predominate as singers and dancers. Religious specialists are typically women, whether they are shamans or simply women who are consistently sought out as ceremonial advisors because of their knowledge about the various rites . . .

"There is no specific age at which women begin to participate in mourning ceremonies, but their interest seems to develop slowly with age. Many young women are openly skeptical about the need for some of the ceremonies. They confess to little interest in them, and they lack the ritual knowledge and skills that their mothers—or grandmothers possess. Standing outside a temple during dugu [a ceremony], watching the older women dance inside, young women and men routinely admit that they do not even understand the meaning of the songs being sung. Most older women, in contrast, are true believers who are well-versed in the large body of belief and protocol [correct behavior], associated with the death rites."[1]

★   ★   ★

Points to Consider

1. What specific things do women do as chief organizers and participators in death rituals of the:
    - mourning
    - visitation and wake
    - burial
    - ninth-night wake-after burial
2. Discuss in your group several reasons why older women might be the major organizers and participants in these death rituals. Give at least four specific reasons why these religious roles are prominent ones for Black Carib women (give evidence to back up your answers). In developing your answers, keep in mind factors such as: the job situation, age, women's roles in the family, and religious beliefs of the Black Caribs.
    After developing your answers, compare them with those of other groups in class discussion.
3. From the evidence here, where might this group fall on the continuum of equity to extreme patriarchy? Does it or does it not seem to apply to them? Explain.
4. Minority groups like the Black Carib may provide some alternative role models from women in the majority culture. In this case, how might women have more leadership roles within their own system of death rituals than in the rituals of the Roman Catholic Church (the religion of both the Black Carib and the majority culture)?

---

[1]These rituals are discussed at length in: Virginia Kerns, *Women and the Ancestors* (Urbana: University of Illinois Press. 1983).

Lidia Gueiler Tejada—AP/Wide World Photos

Chapter 7

Women In Contemporary
Latin America

A. Women's Political Activities—Bureaucrats, Politicians and Protestors

Women involved in politics in Latin American countries have been harassed on occasion because of their political activities. Domitila Barios de Chungara, the wife of a Bolivian miner, was arrested for her involvement in organizing labor strikes. Her jailer threatened to *"work her over."*[1] Women in the Peruvian parliament were from an elite class, but their treatment by politicians was similarly poor. In 1956, in the first election after receiving the vote, nine women were elected to the Peruvian parliament. In the next congress there were only two survivors, partly because of the harassment they received. One woman explained why she did not run for office again:

"Men still are not at all used to the idea of women participating in public life. To men, women still are inferior beings. In my own days in congress, there were all kinds of pressures and, indeed, all kinds of chaffing and even crude joking. 'How does the Sr. (Mr.) like having a legislator in his house? What does he think of your coming home so late?' [The congress in Peru meets in the evenings, and sometimes the sessions go on all night.] 'How does the Sr. like sleeping alone?'"[2]

The implication was that women were out of line to be in politics and that their husbands were weaklings—lacking machismo—to allow them to become involved. A cartoon from a Lima newspaper in the 1960's shows a cowering

---

[1]Domitila Barrios de Chungara, *Let Me Speak!* (New York: London Review Press, 1978), p.119-124.

[2]Elsa Chaney, *Women in Latin American Politics: The Case of Peru and Chile,* unpublished Ph.D. dissertation (University of Wisconsin, 1971), p. 321.

husband with a demanding judge-wife:

LA CARICATURA DE HOY

Fuero de la Mujer

... Y ORDENO QUE TAMBIEN AYUDE A COCINAR Y A LAVAR LOS PAÑALES!

Justicia femenina

...And I order you also to help cook and to wash the diapers!

—*El Comercia*, Lima, Jan. 18, 1967[3]

To protect their families and themselves from such ridicule, some women hesitated to begin political careers. The woman who served as mayor of San Juan, Puerto Rico, for 22 years (from 1946-1968), Felisa Rincon de Gautier, was asked to run for political office twice before she finally decided to campaign. The first time her father asked her not to run; the second time her husband discouraged her from running.[4] Family support is an important factor when women decide to enter politics. A quarter of the women politicians in Colombia have had kinsmen in politics who approved and offered support of their career

choice.[5] No doubt some of them, like the Chilean politician Jorge Alessandri who admitted he only reluctantly voted for his own niece, did not support their female relatives with much enthusiasm.[6] With a male kinsman in politics, a woman politician might seem to be more properly protected.

Besides propriety there were other objections against women becoming politicians. Women were said to be too emotional and unreasonable to be put in positions requiring decision making.[7] For example, the Panamanian Foreign Minister to the United Nations, Jorge Enrique Illueca, blamed Margaret Thatcher's toughness in the Falkland/Malvinas conflict in 1982 to the *"glandular system of women."*[8] If women's glands were not at fault, it was their *"hearts."* Another view expressed against women in politics was that *"politics demands more logic than*

[3]*Ibid.*, p. 251.

[4]Annette Oliveira, "Doña Fela, The Great Lady of Puerto Rican Politics," *Americas* Vol. 33, No. 1 (January 1981), p. 51.

[5]Shirley Harkess and Patricia Finzon de Lewin, "Women, the Vote, and the Party in the Politics of the Colombian National Front," *Journal of Inter-American Studies and World Affairs*, Vol. 17, No. 4 (November 1975), p. 447.

[6]Elsa Chaney, *Supermadre: Women in Politics in Latin America!* (Austin: The University of Texas Press, 1979), p. 87.

[7]Rosemary Brana-Shute, "Women, Clubs and Politics: The Case of a Lower-Class Neighborhood in Paramaribo, Suriname," *Urban Anthropology*, Vol. 5, No. 2 (1976), p. 175.

[8]A.C. Doelling, "Diplomats: Sexism is Major Woe at the U.N.," Minneapolis Star and Tribune (August 15, 1982), p. 3-B. Jean Kirkpatrick, United States Ambassador to the United Nations reminded delegates that the Americas were discovered through Queen Isabella of Spain, another individual with similar glands.

heart; it was a more masculine activity than feminine.''[9]

Perhaps the most frequent criticism of women in politics was that their proper place was in the home. This idea was expressed even by women who eventually became involved in politics. Maria Elena Carrerra de Corbalán, a socialist, ran for her husband's senate seat after his death. But she decided that:

''While my husband lived, I felt I could best make my contribution to the revolution by backing him up, relieving him of home responsibilities, making a tranquil atmosphere for him to come home to.''[10]

Even if women did get elected, family members often expected them to continue home responsibilities. A woman mayor in Brazil found that after her election, her brothers still expected her to stay home from business meetings to care for their aged mother.[11]

Election or appointment to office did not always mean that women politicians would be taken seriously. Sometimes there were so few women in office—only as tokens— that they were easy to freeze out and they had their ideas ignored. One described a meeting of her department:

''The woman in public office or in a profession must be a 'fighter.' There still is very strong discrimination against the professional woman. Today it is perhaps more subtle than before, but it is very strong . . . . My area [in the government] traditionally is considered to be just a cut above the others, and moreover, I was seated next to the Minister. But he called the others (all men) to

speak first. A little thing, certainly, but indicative.''[12]

In a novel, Magda Portal, a leader in the Peruvian *Aprista* party, described her experience as the only woman in the high command. She portrays herself as the novel's character Maria de la Luz:

[María de la Luz] ''holds an important post in the High Command. But meetings devoted to high policy always take place without her. How could one confide in feminine discretion? Maria is too intolerant, too ascerbic, too proud. She is not subservient, she does not adapt to the circumstances. She has intellectual prejudices. She doesn't get on with the leaders' wives because she thinks herself better than they. She doesn't get on with the party leaders because the presence of a woman among so many men shocks them. Moreover, she always sits in judgment. When she makes an appearance in the High Command, they only take up formal business. And when she disagrees, the majority of the Command refute her. She stands alone. Often she leaves the room as a sign of protest, and then all breathe easier.

''They keep Maria de la Luz in the High Command because a woman is necessary in order that no one may accuse the party of

---

[9]Chaney, *Women in Latin America*, p. 286.

[10]Quoted in: *Ibid.*, p. 63.

[11]Eva Alterman Blay, ''The Political Participation of Women in Brazil: Women Mayors,'' *Signs*, Vol. 5, No. 1 (Autumn 1979), p. 57.

[12]Quoted in, Chaney, *Women in Latin America*, p. 75.

Doña Felisa Rincón de Gautier, Mayor of San Juan, Puerto Rico, for 20 years. After a devastating hurricane hit the city, she ran for office as she felt the city government had failed to properly protect people.

excluding women. Moreover, they can't replace her because the other women all lack the prestige and the leadership qualities which she possesses."[13]

Despite all the obstacles, women politicians have played important roles in Latin American politics. They have done so by often using the "Supermadre" model, as described by political scientist Elsa Chaney. The "Supermadre" is a woman politician who stresses her motherly concern for her constituents—those electing her. She does not confront the male world by trying to fit into it. Instead, she carries her domestic role further into the outer world of

politics.[14] Her interest in politics is justified, then, by her social concern. Here, for example, is Mayor Doña Felisa Rincón de Gautier's explanation of her decision to finally run for political office:

"A hurricane hit the island in 1945.

"They announced that the storm was coming and hundreds of people crowded into my apartment because it was very big," Rincón recalled. She provided dry clothes

---

[13]*Ibid.*, p. 299–300.

[14]Chaney, *Supermadre*, p. 22.

and food. She pleaded with island officials to open a building for shelter, but they declined because a disaster had not been officially declared. Refusing to take 'no' for an answer, Rincón marched a few men to a nearby school and asked them to break down the door. *'That was the day that I decided to become mayor,'* she said, *'no matter who might disapprove.'* In December 1946 she was appointed City Manager when the incumbent resigned. *'Now,'* she smiled, *'they give people shelter before the storm breaks. I was the one who changed that.'*[15]

As politicians, women often became involved in social legislation or were appointed to ministries of education or social welfare. A survey of Peruvian and Chilean women officeholders found that 70% were in "feminine" offices such as social welfare or labor ministries.[16] They were largely absent from defense and business agencies. Women are often invited into politics by appeals to their motherly consciences. The following is an appeal for more women to enter politics, by Maria Elena Carrera of the Socialist Party of Chile, made in the early 1970's.

"Women must realize that their work in politics is for the good of their own children and families, being the most remunerative in the emotional sense, through its importance for others and for the country's future."[17]

The "Supermadre" image makes it possible for Latin American women to participate in politics by using the excuse that it is an extension of their domestic concerns. This can be seen in the careers of individual women, like the teachers and social workers who became Brazilian mayors[18] or Mayors Felisa Rincón de Gautier of San Juan and Alicia Canas of Santiago. These domestic concerns, spilling over into political ones, formed part of the political events in Chile during the early 1970's.

The causes of the downfall of President Salvador Allende's government in Chile are complex. Some historians feel that the United States Central Intelligence Agency (CIA) played a role in his being overthrown. Others say that the United States recall of loans caused the economic crisis that led to the military coup. There was also internal dissatisfaction with Allende who was trying to move Chile to a more socialistic form of government. A Brazilian observer, however, felt the turning point came when women began demonstrating against Allende. *"Once we saw the Chilean women were marching, we knew that Allende's days were numbered."*[19]

When he was elected, Salvador Allende knew he was not the first choice of women voters. He got 36.2% of the total votes cast but only 30.5% of women's votes.[20]

[15]Oliveira, "Doña Fela, The Great Lady of Puerto Rico," p. 51-52.

[16]Chaney, *Women in Latin America*, p. 351.

[17]Quoted in, Sandra Carol Thomas, "The Women of Chile and Education for Contemporary Society," unpublished Ph.D. dissertation (St. Louis University, 1973), p. 336.

[18]Blay. "Women Mayors in Brazil," p. 53.

[19]Michele Mattelart, "Chile: The Feminine Version of the Coup D' Etat," in, *Sex and Class in Latin America*, June Nash and Helen Icken Safa, eds., (New York: Praeger, 1976), p. 279.

[20]Maria de los Angeles Crummet, "El Poder Feminino: The Mobilization of Women Against Socialism in Chile," *Latin American Perspectives*, Vol. 4 (Winter/Spring 1977), p. 108.

Allende became president by forming a coalition with other minority parties. He did carry out some reforms aimed at helping women. Mothers' Centers with free distribution of milk to improve mother-child nutrition were created, and land reform programs were meant to encourage women as farmers as well as men.[21] But Allende and his leftist coalition government has been criticized for not building on these early reforms. Criticisms include the following:

- Allende himself was paternalistic in his speech and attitudes towards women. He usually referred to women as *"wives, mothers, girl friends and lovers."*[22]
- Allende ignored women leaders like Vania Bambirra who urged more women's participation.[23] He promised women cabinet appointments but came through with only one—and that a temporary one.
- Socialist journals portrayed women in sexist ways such as in cheesecake poses. Little was done by the government to encourage the idea of women participating in the government as political partners.[24]
- Even women in his own political party expressed the wish not to be assigned to work with women's issues, as these were seen as having low priority.[25]

Perhaps Allende's worst political misjudgment was to underestimate the women who opposed him. Women on the political right who worked against Salvador Allende's leftist coalition government, organized themselves across class lines. They formed a group called *El Poder Feminino* that included women of both the working and middle classes. Their major protests were against economic conditions in Chile. Disruption in the economy caused by new socialist programs and foreign financial pressures had led to serious food shortages. It further appeared to many women that Allende was trying to impose Marxist-Communist ideas which threatened Chilean values that emphasized the importance of the family and Church. Long lines for food—and the rationing which came later—led women to organize the 1971 "March of the Empty Pots." Middle-class women beating on pots mobilized in protest against food shortages in a mass demonstration.

Other organized tactics by women against Allende's government followed:

"Female demonstrators heckled, jeered, and insulted military personnel the interviews revealed. Ms. F explained, 'We wrote letters to Leigh, Merino, and Pinochet (members of the junta) pleading them to save our families from the chaos and violence perpetrated by the UP. In the letters we not only questioned their duty as soldiers, but their virility, their machismo. We put it in very strong terms . . . . We threw wheat in the

[21]Carol Andreas, "The Chilean Woman: Reform, Reaction and Resistance," *Latin American Perspectives*, Vol. 4 (Winter/Spring 1977), p. 121, 124.

[22]Norma Stoltz Chinchilla, "Mobilizing Women: Revolution in the Revolution," in *Women in Latin America, An Anthology*, Eleanor Leacock, et al., (Riverside, California: Latin American Perspectives, 1979), p. 147.

[23]*Ibid.*, p. 147-148.

[24]Elsa Chaney, "The Mobilization of Women in Allende's Chile," in *Women in Politics*, Jane Jaquette, ed., (New York: John Wiley, 1974), p. 271.

[25]Andreas, "The Chilean Woman," p. 124.

soldiers' barracks to imply that they were 'chickens.' Several women also contemplated painting the barracks a light blue color so that "baby boys" would come out. If we had to humiliate them to make them act then we would do so." [26]

- Radio broadcasts directed at women were made daily. One of the people broadcasting against Allende was Juana Castro, half-sister to the Cuban Communist leader Fidel Castro, warning that Chile might become another Cuba. [27]
- Wives of miners put up soup kitchens to demonstrate the bad conditions. [28]
- Anti-Allende songs were written and sung by women's groups.
- More marches were organized and carried out.

Partly because of the pressures brought by women's demonstrations, the Allende government was overthrown by a military coup.

There was irony in the results of the women's demonstrations, since the junta (or military government) which followed Allende has tried to push women out of Chilean politics. The *El Poder Feminino* was disbanded. The junta even outlawed the wearing of slacks by women as a sign that women should not be militant and should assume traditional roles. There has been international concern about the welfare of the women who opposed the military takeover. A large number of women, as well as men, have been listed as "desaparecidos" (disappeared ones). These people are not officially listed as having been arrested, but their fates are unknown. The final outcome for women of the Chilean women's movement of the early 1970's is still

to be learned. The emphasis in these demonstrations by women was upon using long-standing female symbols—the empty pots, soup kitchens and radio broadcasts that combined recipes being read with Juana Castro's political speeches—illustrates how domestic concerns of women could help to unseat a government.

Not all women in Latin America have used the domestic or traditional image of Supermadre to succeed in politics. Especially in the 1960's and 1970's there was a very different image of women who were politically involved, that of women guerrilla fighters. These women took equal chances with men in the violent overthrow of governments. Cuba set the model with women like Haydee Santamaria, Celia Sanchez and Vilma Espin who fought in the guerrilla war against Fulgencio Batista, the Cuban dictator. Perhaps the best known woman guerrilla operator was Haydee Tamara Bunke Bider. An Argentine woman of German-Russian parentage, she became better known as "Tania." She participated in underground activities in Colombia and Bolivia and was killed in guerrilla operations of the pro-Castro guerrilla, Che Guevara. [29]

---

[26]Crummett, "El Poder Feminino," p. 107.

[27]*Ibid.*, p. 106.

[28]Mattelart, "Chile: The Feminine Version of the Coup D' Etat," p. 285.

[29]Tania's career was controversial. One view sees her as a double agent for both Castro and the Soviets who may have deliberately sabotaged Ché Guevara's operation. See Daniel James, ed., *The Complete Bolivian Diaries of Ché Guevara* (New York: Stein and Day, 1968), p. 27. Another view holds that she was not a double agent and her mission failed because of Guevara's mistakes. (James Henderson and Linda Roddy Henderson, *Ten Notable Women of Latin America* (Chicago: Nelson-Hall, 1978), p. 234.

Women protestors at the Plaza de Mayo, Buenos Aires, Argentina

Women were also involved in other guerrilla activities in Colombia, supported by the groups known as *Camilo Torres*.[30] Women active in guerrilla operations in the 1960's and early 1970's included:
Venezuela:
  Elizabeth Burgos
Guatemala:
  Kris Yon Cerna
  Eunice Campiran de Aguila Mora
  Rogelia Cruz Martinez
  Marian Peter Bradford
    (a Mary Knoll nun)
Brazil:
  Sister Maurina Borgha de Silviera
  Yara Spadini
Uruguay:
  Lucia Topolanski
  Marie Esther Giglio[31]
In the 1970's the names of women involved in anti-government activities in countries with military governments or dictatorships became difficult for outsiders to learn. Instead of being publicly arrested and tried, dissenters simply disappeared. This led to the creation of new women's groups in Brazil and Argentina—called *The Mother's Club*—but the reason for their formation is a tragic one. A Brazilian mother described her daughter's arrest:

"One woman, whose daughter was among hundreds of students arrested at her university a few years ago after passing out leaflets critical of the government, told me how her family's life had changed from the moment the soldiers came to her home one morning to arrest the girl.

"The soldiers held machine guns aimed at the younger children. My thirteen-year-old son

[30]See German Guzman, *Camilo Torres* (New York: Sheed and Ward, 1969).

[31]Jane Jaquette, "Women in Revolutionary Movements in Latin America," *Journal of Marriage and the Family*, Vol. 35 (May 1973), p. 348-351.

comforted his sister, 'Don't be afraid, it's only a gun.' 'It's loaded,' warned the soldier. 'Of course, it's loaded,' said Paulo. 'What good would it be if it weren't loaded?' As soon as they left with my daughter, I tore out of the house to get her sister who had already gone off to school. 'You're going into hiding,' I told her. 'Don't ask any questions. If they arrest me, I won't tell them where you are. I may be a coward, but I'm a mother first.' When my arrested daughter was finally released from prison after six days of beatings, electric shocks, and other tortures, she told us how they finally got her to give them a false confession. She heard a girl screaming in the next room and the torturers told her it was her sister; to make them stop, she 'confessed.' If she had only known that I had already hidden her sister! I could do so little—for her or for the others. All I ever did was hide them, help some get away, try to heal them when they were hurt. . . . My children grew up with people like her around. The kids knew what was going on, although I never told them any details. The less you know the less they can torture out of you. But they all knew why these strangers were in our house. And they never talked. Never!'

"This woman had always opposed the policies of the military government but had been frustrated by the way most women she knew either supported them or stood apart from politics. But in 1968, when large numbers of young people disappeared as her daughter had into Brazil's jails, their mothers changed their minds—and their lives. In that year the military rounded up student leaders at the major universities; tortured them for periods ranging from a few days to a few weeks; extracted from them 'confessions' and the names of other 'subversives;' and threw them out on the street without bringing any charges against them. It was an effective deterrent to student protest against any government policy. While these youths were missing—and their families given no information about them—their distraught mothers went to the prisons, to cry, kneel, shout, and demand to know where their children were. The police beat them up and drove them away, but they persisted. They even organized, well enough to persuade the National Council of Catholic Bishops to intervene with the Army, and obtain permission for groups of eight or ten women at a time to visit the prisons to see if their children were there. The visiting mothers were also able to look for other people's children. They got up a newsletter giving the names of arrested people, the names of tortured people, the names of prisoners who had been visited. They gradually built a network of information—and since knowledge is power, have been able to keep some people alive, and to protect some from continued torture. The government seems ordinarily to be much more careful with people who are known to be in its custody.''[32]

---

[32]Joan Myers Weimer, "The Mother, the Macho and the State," *International Journal of Women's Studies*, Vol. 1, No. 1 (January/February 1978), p. 80-81.

Lidia Gueiler Tejada—AP/Wide World Photos

Lidia Gueiler Tejada served as president of Bolivia in 1979

Networks of women in Brazil who try to find out, by silent marches and public witness, what has happened to political prisoners, make powerful use of the image of the suffering mother. But these women are presenting more than an image; they protest in countries where protests have not been allowed. When one woman was asked why she got involved in such dangerous activities, she replied, *"**Nothing radicalizes a person as efficiently as being tortured.**"*[33]

The range of women in Latin American politics has been a wide one, from Eva and Isabel Perón to Tania; from the noisy public "Empty Pot" demonstrators to quiet Lady Mayors. Even in countries with open elections, women are new to voting. Most women in Latin America have

only been given the right to vote in their own lifetime. The following women are new to politics. They can be viewed as exceptions, as Latin American women have had low rates of participation in politics:

- Aida Gonzalez Martinez, Mexican career diplomat and first woman chair of the International Labor Organization of the United Nations.
- Josefina Calcano de Temeltas, Supreme Court Justice in Venezuela.
- Julieta Jardi de Morales Macedo of Uruguay, President of the Inter-American Commission of Women of the Organization of American States.

★   ★   ★

Points to Consider

1. What does social scientist Elsa Chaney mean by the political woman she calls a "Supermadre?" How have Latin American women made it permissible to leave the home and be involved in politics by using the "Supermadre" role?
2. In what ways did Magda Portal and other women elected or appointed to political office feel they were harassed or discriminated against? What reasons were used for excluding women from political jobs?
3. Brazil is not the only Latin American country where women have organized to find missing relatives. Argentina also had an

---

[33]*Ibid.*, p. 81.

oppressive military government that has arrested and imprisoned people without notifying relatives or conducting trials. In 1984 the military government was replaced by a democracy. Some analysts feel that the women who marched in protest in The Plaza de Mayo, in Buenos Aires, the capital of Argentina, helped to bring about the downfall of the military dictatorship.

GRANDMOTHERS OF THE MISSING
From: *HERSAY*,
July 12, 1982

Argentina's Association of Grandmothers is continuing its search for 91 children who disappeared during the political crackdowns of the last decade.

Some of the children were arrested along with their parents. Others were born in concentration camps where the government imprisoned suspected subversives in the late 1970's. Human rights organizations estimate as many as 14,000 Argentine citizens 'disappeared' during those years, and most are now believed dead.

Efforts to trace their children, in most cases, have led nowhere . . .

The Los Angeles Times says the grandmothers association keeps records on the missing grandchildren, and continues to visit government offices and courthouses, seeking their missing sons' and daughters' missing offspring.'' [34]

Why might an organization of grandmothers that demonstrates against these arrests be particularly effective against military regimes?

How might these women use the idea of machismo to work against military regimes and to make their demonstrations more effective.

4. One socialist idea is to free women from domestic tasks so they can work outside the home. As a socialist, Salvador Allende might have been expected to approve of wider roles for women. And yet groups of women organized against Allende and finally aided in his downfall. What mistakes did Allende seem to make with his women constituents? Although Allende believed in equality for women, what showed that he did not really accept women as equals? Why did the women of *El Poder Feminino* organize against him? How were their empty pots a symbol of the issue particularly important to them?

---

[34]Quoted in, Fran P. Hosken, *WIN News*, Vol. 8, No. 3 (Summer 1982), p. 73.

Group Exercise—
The Case of Venezuela

5. Look over the following data and then answer the questions that follow:

Population: 14,700,000
Literacy rates: 80% males
                73% females
President elected for five years

Venezuela:
Women in Government and Leadership Positions

Women in Venezuela, in recent years, have obtained more leadership positions than in most other countries around the world. Some of the prominent women in Venezuela occupy the following positions:

Minister of State for the Participation of Women in Development:
Mercedes Pulido de Briceno

Justice of the Venezuela Supreme Court:
Josefina Calcano de Temeltas

Minister of State for Planning:
Marzita Izaguirre Porras

Minister of Agriculture:
Nydia Villegas de Rodriquez

Minister of Urban Development:
Maria Cristina Maldonado Gil de Campos Rodriquez

Minister of State for Parliamentary Affairs:
Leonor Mirabal Manrique

Governor, State of Trujillo:
Dora Maria Maldonado Mancera de Falcon

Chairwoman of the Sociedad Financiera Industrial de Venezuela, C.A.:
Olga Ferrer de Hernandez

Dr. Haydee Martinez de Osorio of Venezuela, Director of the National Institute for Children, was appointed chair of an important branch of the United Nations (UNICEF) Executive Board in December 1983.

President of the Industrial Credit Fund (Fondo de Credito Industrial): Raiza Bortone Alcala

President, Foundation for Community Development and Municipal Improvement:
Alba Cecilia Illaramendi Acevedo

Superintendent of Consumer Protection Office:
Migdalia Garcia Rodriquez

President, National Institute of Parks: Zoraida Irazabal[35]

---

[35]Quoted in, Fran P. Hosken, *WIN News*, Vol. 9, No. 1 (Winter 1983), p. 61.

Venezuela has been an oil exporting country and the richest country in Latin America for about ten years. This has meant an expanding economy. And with industrial growth, more trained people were needed. Why might these circumstances further the chances for some groups of women to expand their options from the traditional home ones to the possibility of occupations outside the home? What groups of women might be the ones to have expanded opportunities?

At least until very recently, it would probably be difficult to make as long a list of women in powerful government positions in the United States as those listed in *Venezuela: Women in Government and Leadership Positions.* Yet the United States has a higher rate of literate women, and United States women have had the vote longer (1918) than women in Venezuela (1947). Why might a country whose economy has expanded very quickly have more women involved in government? How might the rather severe class system be an aid to certain women in gaining government positions?

Look over the list of appointments or positions that Venezuelan women government leaders hold. Which of them are feminine ones in the sense of being extensions of caretaking and domestic concerns? Which are traditionally masculine ones— oriented toward business, foreign affairs, law or technology? How might a Latin American society that highly values the family and motherhood help to explain women's appointments to certain positions of the government? How do you explain the exceptions?

B. Modern Cuba—Has there been a Revolution for Women?

Background Information

During the decades from the 1960's to the 1980's relations between Cuba and the United States have generally been hostile. Many Cuban refugees came to the United States to protest the rule of Fidel Castro and the socialization of the Cuban economy. The United States supported an unsuccessful armed attack by Cuban refugees on Cuba at the Bay of Pigs in 1961. The closest the United States and the Soviet Union have come to nuclear war was over the placing of Soviet missiles in Cuba in 1962. With this serious antagonism to each other, it is somewhat ironic that in this same 20-year period Cuba and the United States have been the two countries in the Americas most concerned with women's rights.

Women's rights movements in the two countries have shared some of the same aims: more equal education for girls when compared with boys, fairer recognition of women's work, more job opportunities for women and equity in legal rights. But the means for achieving these ends were different. Women in the United States met in small "consciousness raising" groups at the grass-roots level and later formed larger voluntary organizations like NOW (National Organization of Women), WEAL (Women's Equity Action League) and other groups.[1] The United States women's movement could look back on some real gains for women and some failures by the l980's. One 12-month period saw the first women appointed to the Supreme Court of the United States

---

[1]Oscar Lewis, Ruth Lewis and Susan Rigdon, *Four Women: Living the Revolution: An Oral History of Contemporary Cuba* (Urbana: University of Illinois Press, 1977), p. x-xii.

and the defeat of the Equal Rights Amendment to the Constitution.

Changes for women in Communist Cuba since the Castro revolution have not come from the grass roots, but rather were imposed from the top down. There were women feminists in Cuba who wanted changes made and who helped get the vote for women in 1935. The leader of the *Federation of Cuban Women*, created by the Castro government as the major organization for women, was not one of these feminists. Vilma Espin, wife of Castro's brother Raul, had been a chemical engineer before becoming involved in revolutionary activities. In 1959 Castro asked her to organize the *Federation of Cuban Women*. She later commented on her appointment:

"I asked precisely why do we have to have a women's organization? I had never been discriminated against. I had my career as a chemical engineer. I never suffered, I never had any difficulty."[2]

Vilma Espin, who headed the *Federation of Cuban Women*, saw no reason for even having a women's organization. The person, then, most influential in the recent women's rights movement in Cuba has been a man—Fidel Castro.

The position of Castro on a particular women's issue, however, has been dependent on how the change would fit the needs of Communist Cuba. The ideal society is seen as one where all people, working together, build a country where economic and political equality exists. This requires that women be more involved in the labor force; campaigns have been carried on to encourage women to work

outside the home. For there to be equity, occupations—like those of domestic servants—had to be eliminated because these were seen as jobs that exploited particular groups of poor women. In the early 1960's the reforms were instrumental in setting up training schools so women could learn sewing and textile work. Their work would be given dignity because it was skilled labor. The desire to encourage equality meant that Castro criticized the machismo ideal. At a 1974 women's conference, Fidel Castro said that more women leaders were needed because, *"We need a government of men and women, a party of men and women, a central committee of men and women."*[3]

In reviewing the changes in women's legal and educational status in Cuba since the Communists came to power in 1959, Castro's "top-down" approach has made some real progress:

- One-half of the medical students at the universities are women.
- Literacy rates for women have increased.
- The percentage of women in the labor force has increased from 14.2% in 1958 to 25.3% in 1975.
- Government child care centers have been opened to aid working mothers.

---

[2]Quoted in, Max Azicri, "Women's Development Through Revolutionary Mobilization: A Study of the Federation of Cuban Women," *International Journal of Women's Studies*, Vol. 2, No. 1 (January/February 1979), p. 29.

[3]Quoted in, Margaret Randall, "'We Need a government of Men and Women!,'" in *Women in Latin America*, Eleanor Leacock, et al., (Riverside, Calforina: Latin America Perspectives, 1979), p. 138.

- Explanation of the revised 1974 Family Code stressed the need for both men and women to take part in housework and child care chores.

Haydee Santamaria was one of the original group of Cuban guerrillas with Castro from the beginning of the revolution. She is now a member of the Central Committee of the Cuban Communist Party. She summarized the effect of the Cuban Revolution:

"HAYDEE: It's hard for me to talk about that, but the first step the Revolution has taken towards women liberating themselves is support. A woman must have economic support. Because how many women used to stay with a man and not leave him because if she left him what would she give her children to eat? How would it be for her children? And the poorest would say: 'What am I going to give my children to eat?' The Revolution has emancipated women economically; it pays them the same salaries it pays men. It doesn't pay her for being a woman, but for the job she does. If she does the same work as a man they both get the same pay; if it's a lower-paid job, they both make less. And this has been a tremendous liberation for women. Her children have their school, their formation. A lot of women from the middle or upper classes didn't have this problem, but here girls were raised to 'marry a little bit better.' That was the way it was. And with the boys, too, women would say: 'What am I going to do with my son without his father? When he's fourteen he's going to go astray!' And today that mother puts her son in a boarding school and he gets a complete education there. It's not that I'm saying I don't think the mother and father are necessary, and when I say mother and father I mean the feminine figure and the masculine figure."[4]

Notice how her description stresses the economic needs and work roles of women. Cuba has been praised for opening more work opportunities for women than most Latin American countries have allowed. But Cuba has been criticized for limiting changes and reforms for women to those which fit the needs of the state, especially those that have aided women entering the work force.[5] When food rationing was put into effect in the 1960's, long lines made grocery shopping time consuming, and women began to drop out of the labor force. The government then kept stores open longer and allowed working women to shop at special times.[6] Changes that will help women to work outside the home and contribute to a socialist state are the ones supported by the government - not necessarily ones that will improve the status of women.[7]

[4]Quoted in Margaret Randall, *Cuban Women Now* (Toronto: The Women's Press, 1974), p. 317.

[5]Susan Kaufman Purcell, "Modernizing Women for a Modern Society: The Cuban Case," in *Female and Male in Latin America*, Ann Pescatello, ed., (Pittsburgh: University of Pittsburgh Press, 1973), p. 259.

[6]Lourdes Casal, "Revolution and Conciencia: Women in Cuba," in *Women, War and Revolution*, Carol Berkin and Clara Lovett, eds., (New York: Holmes and Meier, 1980), p. 193.

[7]*Ibid.*, p. 193.

Group Exercise

In groups of four to six students, after appointing a recorder, look over the following list of criticisms of Castro's Cuba concerning the role of women. As a group you are going to try to consider each criticism the way it might be viewed in Communist Cuba. Answer these questions about each of the criticisms:

1. Would a change or reform advance the cause of women's equality within the framework of Communism?
2. Would adopting such a reform endanger the state (Cuba) causing Communist Cuba to reject the change or reform?

Decide whether you think the Communist Cuban government would *A* (advance) or *R* (reject) the necessary reforms meant to correct each problem. Then give a brief reason for your group's decision.

1. **Criticism:**
   Castro's Cuba has only had *"consciousness raising"* groups led by party leaders. Women cannot learn to be individuals without organizing their own groups.
   Reform:
   Women would form separate groups to discuss areas of inequity to men.

2. **Criticism:**
   The Central Committee of the Cuban Communist Party in 1976 had only six women out of a total of 100. No women serve on the important Political Bureau of the Party. The Cuban Communist Party has about 12% women members. Cuba is *"still a man's game"* politically.[8]
   Reform:
   More women should be encouraged to gain political power and be appointed to the powerful Central Committee and Political Bureau.

3. **Criticism:**
   Studies show that most Cuban men do not help their working wives at home (much less share chores equally). One study showed that Cuban working women have 2 hours, 42 minutes free time per day, while men have 4 hours, 4 minutes.[9]
   Reform:
   More equality in domestic duties is needed and should be strongly encouraged by government incentives.

4. **Criticism:**
   While Castro criticizes the macho image in his speeches, he dresses in guerrilla khaki, is unmarried, has no children and is known for his interest in men's game sports. Few public images are given of men in feminine roles.
   Reform:
   Show men doing domestic and child care activities, have role models that are less macho among the government leaders.

5. **Criticism:**
   Vilma Espin, Castro's sister-in-law, has been the only director of the *Federation of Cuban Women*. She has not been particularly interested in women's concerns.
   Reform:
   Democratic elections among rival candidates would make the

[8]Petur Gudjonsson, "Women in Castro's Cuba," *The Progressive*, Vol. 36 (August 1972), p. 29.

[9]Azicri, "Women's Development Through Revolutionary Mobilization," p. 38.

Federation better reflect women's views.

6. **Criticism:**
Women who have government positions have been assigned to supervise areas such as light industry or education, which were traditionally women's occupations.[10] Women should also be represented in other government areas like the military and business positions.
Reform:
Appoint women to a variety of cabinet and government posts—especially non-traditional ones.

7. **Criticism:**
Virtually no men work in Cuban child care centers or as teachers in primary grades. The social practice of seeing these occupations as women's roles continues.[11]
Reform:
Provide government incentives for men to enter these occupations. Encourage their participation with an advertising campaign that pictures men in these positions.

8. **Criticism:**
Posters at rallies celebrating the revolution are almost entirely composed of male guerrilla leaders. One exception sometimes shown is Tamara Bunke, an Argentine woman whose family came from East Germany and who died in Bolivia.[12] Many women fought for the Cuban Revolution and yet their pictures are not seen.
Reform:
Give prominence to women active in the revolution both in the histories of Cuba and at rallies celebrating the revolution.

9. **Criticism:**
Even garment workers' unions, which are made up mostly of women, elect men to represent them at bargaining sessions. They do so because they think men get more respect.[13]
Reform:
Train selected women to participate in collective bargaining sessions. Put on training workshops in assertiveness for women garment workers.

10. **Criticism:**
The government publishes a journal for women called *Mujeres* (Women). One issue analyzed contained a total of 98 pages; 40 pages were devoted to fashions and 13 to recipes. Less than half were devoted to more critical issues for women, and interests other than domestic ones were not suggested as alternatives for women.[14]
Reform:
Include discussions on political, economic and social concerns of women in the journal, alter the format and hire new editors.

[10]Benigno Aguirre, "Women in the Cuban Bureaucracies," in *Women in the Family and the Economy*, George Kurian and Ratna Ghosh, eds., (Westport: Greenwood, 1981), p. 381-387.

[11]Casal, "Revolution and Conciencia," p. 197.

[12]Lewis, Lewis, and Rigdon, *Four Women*, p. xxi.

[13]Inger Holt-Seeland, *Women of Cuba* (Westport: Lawrence Hill, 1981), p. 62.

[14]Azicri, "Women's Development Through Revolutionary Mobilization," p. 31.

Points to Consider

1. In your group, add up your A's (those that advance the cause of women) and R's (those that reject the reform or change). Compare your conclusions and reasons for deciding whether Cuba's Communist government would advance or reject particular reforms for women with other groups in the class.

2. After looking over Cuban policies toward women and deciding which might be reformed under a Communist system, how would your group see changes brought about for Cuban women?

3. Fidel Castro has suggested that reforms are so extensive that the total change represents a *"revolution within a revolution."* Does your group agree that reforms have meant a fundamental change for women? Give examples to defend your position.

C. Working Women—New Opportunities and Old Restrictions

"They lived, they made tortillas, and they died." In this way women of the 1916 Feminist Congress in Mexico described the lives of most Latin American women.[1] The statement may have given a sense of the daily round of chores for women but even in the early 20th century it hardly described the wide variety of possible occupations for women. Travelers to Latin America described women weavers, textile workers, potters, market vendors, and in many other occupations. The phrase, however, does show that the expected place for most Latin American women of all classes was in the home. This view has had a major effect on the employment patterns of women in Latin America.

In trying to compile accurate statistics on working women, researchers are generally in a quandary. They must decide such questions as who should be counted as working, and especially,

should housewives be counted? Women's domestic labor, doing chores like processing food or taking care of children, fulfills basic needs of society and if women's labor had to be hired for wages, would cost dearly. Certainly these women are working women. This unpaid home labor, however, is not counted in the GNP (Gross National Product) as contributing to the country's economy. Women who work outside their homes are generally included in the GNP and are referred to as economically active or as women in the labor force. Even then, women who work in the informal marketplace—such as selling home crafts or working in

---

[1]Quoted in, Mary Elmendorf, "Mexico: The Many Worlds of Women," *Women: Roles and Status in Eight Countries*, Janet Zollinger Giele and Audrey Chapman Smock, eds., (New York: John Wiley, 1977), p. 135.

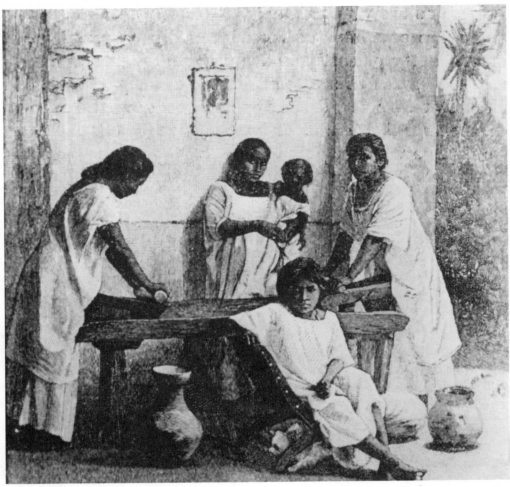

Women grinding corn for tortillas

the fields with their husbands—often are not counted in statistics as being economically active. Statistics on working women are, therefore, very difficult to decipher. Especially in Latin America, where much of women's labor is done informally in the home, the statistics probably do not reflect the extent of their contributions.

The following chart of figures about economically active women compiled by the United Nations in 1980 may suggest some comparisons between different parts of Latin America.

Region or Country	Total Women Mid-1980 (millions)	Women as Percent of Total Labor Force, 1980	Employed Women in Agriculture, 1975 (percent)
LATIN AMERICA	**384**	**23**	**32**
Middle America	**45**	**19**	**3**
Costa Rica	1.1	21	4
El Salvador	2.4	20	8
Guatemala	3.5	14	7
Honduras	1.9	14	4
Mexico	33.9	19	0.3
Nicaragua	1.3	22	5
Panama	1.0	26	8
Carribean	**15**	**38**	**28**
Bahamas	0.1	—	—
Barbados	0.1	40	16
Cuba	4.9	21	12
Dominica	.2	—	—
Dominican Republic	2.7	12	9
Grenada	0.1	—	—
Haiti	3.0	47	58
Jamaica	1.1	38	4
Netherland Antilles	0.1	—	—
Puerto Rico	1.8	29	—
St. Lucia	0.1	—	—
Trinidad and Tobago	0.6	31	16
Tropical South America	**99**	**23**	**14**
Bolivia	2.7	21	22
Brazil	61.2	23	17
Colombia	13.3	25	3
Ecuador	4.0	21	16
Guyana	0.4	25	13
Paraguay	1.6	23	12
Peru	8.8	23	16
Suriname	0.2	27	15
Venezuela	6.9	24	2
Temperate South America	**21**	**26**	**3**
Argentina	13.6	26	4
Chile	5.7	25	2
Uruguay	1.5	29	2
NORTH AMERICA	**126**	**38**	**1**
Canada	12.1	34	2
United States	114.1	38	0.4

[2]

[2]World's Women Data Sheet of the Population Reference Bureau, Inc. in collaboration with UNICEF, April, 1980.

These conclusions are suggested by this chart:
- The Caribbean Islands, especially those not controlled by Spain in colonial times, have patterns of women's economic activities similar to the United States and Canada.
- Latin American countries (that were controlled by Spain and Portugal) seem to have lower levels of women in the outside labor force than those of other

then drop out of the labor force, are no longer economically active. Women in other Western countries reach their major employment periods after their children might be expected to be in school, when women are between the ages of 45-54. These statistics suggest that the women in all areas are in charge of child care and homemaking as they enter and leave the work force in a way men would not. The statistics indicate

FEMALE WORK ACTIVITY BY AGE GROUPS [3]						
	Age group (years)					
Type and country	15-19	20-24	25-44	45-54	55-65	65 and over
Type I: More developed countries in Europe other than Eastern Europe	48.8	61.6	39.4	42.2	34.2	8.4
Japan	50.3	66.4	44.1	45.3	34.2	15.2
Canada	38.5	54.2	33.3	37.2	25.6	7.3
United States	30.8	48.3	41.6	50.3	38.3	11.3
Type II: Latin American countires	27.9	34.9	30.5	25.2	17.7	9.4
Less developed countries in Europe other than Eastern Europe	36.2	41.5	25.9	19.4	14.0	5.9

Western countries (United States, Canada and Europe).
- Argentina, Chile and Uruguay, areas which are racially homogeneous and have more European ties, have higher work rates for women.

The following chart compares the age groups of women working outside the home in city areas and shows another pattern of the women's labor force in Latin America:

This chart shows that Latin American women are at their peak employment from ages 20-24. Many

differences in attitudes and opportunities for married women workers, depending on which world area is studied.

The idea of women working outside the home has not been an acceptable one to all classes in Latin America. Surveys of husbands from the economically lower class have suggested that they, in

[3]Chart from, Ettore Denti, "Sex-Age Patterns of Labour Force Participation by Urban and Rural Population," International Labour Review, Vol. 98, No. 6 (December 1968), p. 539.

particular, see a working wife reflecting badly on their ability to care for their families.[4] Upper-class families also considered it a reflection of family status for women to work. Sometimes historical forces changed these attitudes. The Mexican Revolution disrupted old class systems; newly impoverished families depended on women working at wage jobs.[5] In the 20th century there has been an influx of capital to build manufacturing plants in parts of Latin America, as when the French financed textile industries in Mexico and, more currently, United States capital was used to build factories in Guatemala. New factories made jobs available to women in industries that were traditionally women's work, such as weaving and spinning. The demands of World War II also opened up jobs for women in defense industries in Brazil and broke down some barriers for women.[6] These job opportunities were considered, however, to be suitable primarily for young, single women.

How did Latin American societies treat these single women working outside their homes, no longer protected by their families? In the 1930's young women wore mantillas (black lace head scarves) to their jobs to make it look as if they were going to morning mass at Church instead of out to work.[7] Fathers would meet their daughters after work and see them home. In the 1930's one woman was even met by her fiance and her father. Another had her grandmother escort her home after her job as a waitress.[8] Some factories paid for special segregated buses for women workers to travel to and from their jobs. Even today, studies

of factories in some areas of Brazil and Mexico show that single women tend to work where they have family kin[9] or where family networks of information lead them.[10]

These single women workers are generally expected to live at home or with relatives. A researcher from the United States, Elsa Chaney, found that even single, professional women, doctors and lawyers were expected to live with family:

"A seemingly small but often mentioned detail of current custom illustrates the above attitude. In Lima and in most cases in Santiago, a single woman—no matter what her age, professional status and official position—cannot live alone if she cares about her reputation. In over a year in the former city, with many inquiries and following up of leads on this point, I

---

[4]There are many studies which support this view, but one shows that even among poor families in Mexico City, if a working man is part of the family, the wife was discouraged from working. Lydia Morris, "Women in Poverty: Domestic Organization Among the Poor of Mexico City," *Anthropological Quarterly* (1981), p. 119.

[5]Fanchón Royer, "Working Women of Mexico," *Americas*, Vol. 6, No. 2 (October 1949), p. 168.

[6]Julia Flanigan Suggs, "Women Workers in Brazil," *Phylon*, Vol. 7, No. 1 (1947), p. 62-63.

[7]Mary Cannon, "Women's Organizations in Ecuador, Paraguay and Peru," *Bulletin of the Pan American Union*, Vol. 77, No. 11 (November 1943), p. 606.

[8]Royer, p. 171-172.

[9]Neuma Aguiar, "Impact of Industrialization on Women's Roles in North East Brazil," *Studies in Comparative International Development* (Summer 1975), p. 86.

[10]Lourdes Arizpe and Josefina Aranda, "The 'Comparative Advantages' of Women's Disadvantages: Women Workers in the Strawberry Export Agribusiness of Mexico," *Signs*, Vol. 7, No. 2 (Winter 1981), p. 468.

discovered only one young unmarried professional who had her own apartment—and lived in it. When one finally has some friends 'de confianza' one learns about an interesting alternative— the 'penthouse.' Girls joke among themselves that if their families do not let up on the supervision or permit this or that freedom, 'I'm going to get my penthouse.' This is, of course, not anything so pretentious as the name suggests, but a secret apartment where a girl can decorate to suit her own tastes, keep books and records and receive trusted friends. But she does not sleep there; she locks up and goes 'home' to her father's house and the existence of the apartment never is revealed to family or relatives."[11]

Single women have pressures and restrictions placed on them when they work outside the home, but married women may have even more. In a study of Chilean women workers, almost 50% of the women who wanted to work said their families had negative views about their having jobs away from home.[12] According to one researcher, ***"The Mexican woman who works outside the home, especially if she is married, does so with a guilt complex. She believes that 'women's place is in the home' and that 'her natural mission is to be a wife and mother.'***[13] Working women often feel they must defend themselves from charges of neglecting their families and female home duties. A social worker in Chile in the 1940's reassured her interviewer, ***"I spend more time with [my children] than many society women do."***[14]

Cecilia Davila, a business woman executive in Ecuador

In recent years there has been a new view that professional women should use their training and continue their careers after marriage. Their level of education is one of the major factors in encouraging some women to stay in

[11]Elsa Chaney, "Women in Latin American Politics: The Case of Peru and Chile," unpublished Ph.D. dissertation, University of Wisconsin (1971), p. 67-68.

[12]Sandra Carol Thomas, "The Women of Chile and Education for a Contemporary Society: A Study of Chilean Women, Their History and Present Status and the New Demands of a Society in Transition," unpublished Ph. D. dissertation, Saint Louis University (1973), p. 72.

[13]Maria del Carmen Elu de Lenero, "Women's Work and Fertility," in *Sex and Class in Latin America*, June Nash and Helen Icken Safa, eds., (New York: Praeger, 1976), p. 54.

[14]Erna Fergusson, *Chile* (New York: Knopf, (1943), p. 272

the labor force. And as a group, these women have fewer than average children. These married, professional women sometimes wear themselves out trying to combine the demands of their careers and family duties. One researcher doing a study on professional women in Buenos Aires, Argentina, found that the only free time some of these women had to be interviewed by her was after 10:00 p.m.[15] Many of these women were, however, proud of their husbands' support of their careers and of their own energy in combining both work and home tasks. One lawyer described her pregnancy:

"I was trying my first case before the Supreme Court and I felt something go bang! Can you imagine not just in court but my first case in the Supreme Court! Things were really touch and go. But I patted my tummy, timed the contractions, said some quick Hail Marys, and won the case. I made a swift exit. When my colleagues found out when the baby was born, I was really the heroine of the day."[16]

Married professional women—and their husbands—have felt that women's careers should be in areas thought of as traditionally feminine ones, such as teaching or social work. Until fairly recently, nursing was looked down upon as rather indecent and not a proper career for women. In the early 20th century an argument against women becoming doctors was that they would have to go out at night to treat their patients. Many of these arguments are no longer made, but job discrimination against women continues to exist. For example, in some areas of Brazil, 90% of the women in public jobs were either teachers or nurses.[17] Women professionals may be married, but it is considered important for them to have what is seen as proper careers. It is also important that their careers and salaries should not be more successful or exceed those of their husbands'. As one white-collar worker said when asked whether a woman should work, *"She should work, yes—as long as she keeps her woman's place, not higher than men's."*[18]

If the correct place of the professional woman worker is seen in the fields of social service, the most frequent occupation of lower-class women is that of domestic servant. Most of these servants fit the profile of Latin American women workers. They are usually both young and single. The people they work for become substitute families, so they live within the protection of a family unit and not what was seen as dangerously alone. The adult members of the household they work for are expected to act as their guardians. In many urban areas, the number of women working as servants is substantial. For example, Lima, Peru, in 1970

---

[15]Nora Scott Kinzer, "Women Professionals in Buenos Aires," in *Female and Male in Latin America*, Ann Pescatello, ed., (Pittsburgh: University of Pittsburgh Press, 1973), p. 161.

[16]*Ibid.*, p. 173.

[17]Elizabeth Jelin, "The Bahiana in the Labor Force in Salvador, Brazil," in *Sex and Class in Latin America*, Nash and Safa, eds., p. 139.

[18]Jorge Gissi Bustos, "Mythology About Women, With Special Reference to Chile," in *Sex and Class in Latin America*, Nash and Safa, eds., p. 42.

had 90,000 domestic women workers.[19] Many of these young women who work as servants in Latin American cities are migrants from rural areas.

There are essentially two views which emerge of what it is like to be a domestic servant. The first is that it is a hard life in which workers are expected to work long hours for very little pay and under constant direction from their employer. The second view is that although domestic work is difficult, it does provide a period of socialization for rural young women. The next paragraph tells of the life of a servant woman in Ecuador in the 1960's and represents the first view of domestic work:

"If there is one servant, she works from daybreak till late at night and sometimes until very early the next morning. She builds the cooking fires, makes breakfast, feeds the children, dresses them, washes dishes, takes the children to the school bus, makes the beds, cleans the house, goes shopping for the daily food and prepares all meals, washes and irons the clothes (usually without a washing machine or hot water), tends the children, pays the monthly bills downtown, shops for household items when they are needed, builds the evening fire, and babysits. She runs out with milk bottles or pail when the milkman arrives; goes to the local grocery for the newspaper, bread, soft drinks, and whatever little items she has forgotten on her daily trip to the open market; she sweeps the yard and tends the ever-present animals, including dogs, cats, and poultry; and she carries the garbage to the gate when the truck comes to pick it up. Moreover she runs to the gate to unlock it whenever any member of the household wants to leave or arrives home in wet or dry weather. She makes at least three trips a day out of the house, to escort children to the school or bus, to make purchases, and to run errands, such as carrying mail to the post office because there are no mail boxes or because mail delivery is uncertain. Since there are no telephone deliveries from the downtown stores, she is the one who runs down to buy small items and who returns the children's clothes to the seamstress if the fit is wrong, which it always is, etc. Of course, in the wealthier and larger households, there is a corps of servants among whom these tasks are divided. Servants do not do much more than the average North American housewife, but they operate in a system which is not geared to efficiency or equipped with machinery."[20]

It is no wonder that some women quit these jobs and return to the rural areas from which they came. As one said:

"I was in Lima once for two years working for a family. I had to do everything—cook, wash the clothes, clean the house, take care of my children as well as those of the mistress, do all the

---

[19]Margo L. Smith, "Domestic Service as a Channel or Upward Mobility of the Lower Class Woman: The Lima Case," in *Female and Male in Latin America*, Pescatello, ed., p. 193.

[20]Emily Nett, "The Servant Class in a Developing Country: Ecuador," *Journal of Inter-American Studies*, Vol. 8 (July 1966), p. 441-442.

shopping and account for the money she gave me. I didn't get any salary; they paid me with old clothes for my children and myself, with meals and a little room on the roof. I don't want that life again. We work hard here, too, but at least what we do is for ourselves.''[21]

Though some go back to rural areas, many women choose to remain in the cities as servants.

Recent studies have shown that although the work may be hard, this work experience is also a socialization period for country women.[22] A young rural woman learns many skills necessary for urban living while working for a family. One of these skills may be to learn Spanish, as her own language may be one of the many indigenous ones. She could learn to handle financial transactions and have city shopping experiences. She would also see a more affluent style of life. Although the servant woman may not be able to earn money to live as her employers do, she often saves money and expects her children to live in more affluence than she.[23] Being a domestic servant may not be the dead-end job that it was formerly thought to be. It may rather be a stage in a country woman's education and career in which she gains new skills and ideas to put to use with her own family.

Domestic workers make up the largest percentage of Latin American women workers, but there are also many factory jobs for women. In the early 20th century, particularly in Mexico and Argentina, textile factories had high percentages of women workers, and garment industries still mainly employ women. At the turn of the

Doña Felicitas Charo, a Mayan Mexican in the Yucatan who became a labor leader, struggling against poor working conditions for agricultural laborers.

century, some factories were notorious as sweatshops, with dangerously foul air, over-crowded working quarters, hazardous open fires for heating flat irons and unsanitary, inadequate restroom facilities.[24] Even in the 1970's there were complaints of sexual harassment of women workers by

[21]Quoted in, *Latin American Women: The Meek Speak Out*, June Turner, ed. (Silver Spring: International Education Development, 1980), p. 49.

[22]Nett, ''The Servant Class in a Developing Country: Ecuador,'' p. 445.

[23]Smith, ''Domestic Service as a Channel of Upward Mobility of the Lower Class Woman,'' p. 206.

[24]Nancy Hollander, ''Women in the Political Economy in Argentina,'' unpublished Ph.D. dissertation, University of Calfornia, Los Angeles (1974), p. 106-209.

male supervisors and bad working conditions, even though most countries have labor laws which aim to curb these abuses.

One current issue (especially found within the textile industries and agribusiness in northern Mexico, Central America and the Caribbean) is the influence of multinational corporations on the lives of Latin American working women. Foreign capital, from the United States or elsewhere, has been what is called migratory by economists, meaning it can go where the source of cheapest labor is to be found. Since there are few job opportunities for women in most developing countries, Latin America is a place where certain factories have been built by migratory capital investments. In some ways pools of untapped women's labor are an advantage for countries wanting to attract foreign capital, for example, the new strawberry packing plants of the 1970's built in Lamora, a town in northern Mexico. These plants now employ around 10,000 young women, about 60% of whom never worked before.[25] Their parents, as well as the local Roman Catholic priest, were originally against women working. But the wages that the women earned have changed the standard of living for the town and made more consumer goods available. The townspeople and priest now see the women working in a more positive way.

Many people in developing countries have criticized corporations for taking advantage of Latin American women's working patterns. Businesses rely on women quitting their jobs when they marry. This turnover of workers means that labor unions' organizing efforts are ineffective. Workers do not build seniority rights, and wages continue to be low. Workers sometimes try to form unions as some Caribbean women did against Town and Country, a subsidiary of Sears, Roebuck and Co. But in that case, the amount of unemployed women in the area was so high that 500 workers who went on strike were replaced with new women workers.[26] There have also been complaints that these companies use chemicals and other materials labeled dangerous to workers' health which are not permitted in United States industry.[27] Guatemalan women reported that insecticides were sprayed on them as they were working in cotton fields.[28] Women may be more willing than men to put up with terrible working conditions because they see their jobs as temporary as they expect to stop working after marriage. They may also feel that protests do little good. If an area has too much union agitation, migratory capital will be moved to a new area and other female workers will be hired. Cheap female labor in any particular place generally means lost jobs elsewhere.

[25]Arizpe and Aranda, "The Comparative Advantages of Women's Disadvantages, Women Workers in the Strawberry Export Agribusiness of Mexico," p. 453-456.

[26]Gloria I. Joseph, "Caribbean Women: The Impact of Race, Sex and Class," in *Comparative Perspectives of Third World Women*, Beverly Lindsay, ed., (New York: Praeger, 1980), p. 150.

[27]Devon Gerardo Pena, "'Las Maquiladoras:' Mexican Women and Class Struggle in the Border Industries," *AZTLAN*, Vol. 11, No. 2 (1981), p. 189.

[28]Alicia Herrera, "Testimonies of Guatemalan Women," *Latin American Perspectives*, Vol. 37, Nos. 2-3 (Spring/Summer 1980), p. 161.

The three categories of Latin American women workers considered here—professional, domestic servant and factory worker—do not exhaust all the kinds of women workers. There are Guatemalan women weavers who continue to weave cloth in their homes even though they are elderly. One weaver said, *"I cannot sit around doing nothing and I enjoy weaving."*[29] Women work with their husbands as shepherds in Peru. Zhandra Rodriguez is the leading ballerina of the New World Ballet of Caracas, Venezuela. There have been a few women bullfighters. In 1982 The International Labor Organization of the United Nations elected Aida Gonzalez Martinez of Mexico the first woman chair of their governing body. Her election indicates the high level of involvement of Latin American women in the labor force.[30] The occupations of Latin American women have varied, but the general profile of those economically active suggests that some Latin American women may not have had the employment opportunities they might have wanted.

★   ★   ★

Points to Consider

1. What areas of Latin America have the highest work rates for women?

    In most Latin American countries the percentage of women in agricultural work is quite low. What countries are exceptions to that?

2. According to the 1980 United States census:

    Total population of farm laborers—2.7% are employed in agriculture (2,750,000)

    Total farms—2,428,000

    Women farm owners—128,000 farms (women are sole owners or principal operators) (5%)

    Total women in agriculture—1.1% of total women in labor force

    List specific things you notice about women farmers in the United States.

    Compare your list with things you noticed about women farmers in Latin America.

    For what reasons might the United States statistics on women farmers not actually show many women who work on farms as laborers or as farm operators?

    Would this be true in Latin America as well?

[29]Quoted in, Lois Paul, "The Mastery of Work and the Mystery of Sex in a Guatemalan Village," in *Woman Culture and Society*, Michelle Rosaldo and Louise Lamphere, eds., (Stanford: Stanford University Press, 1974), p. 286.

[30] ILO Information Bulletin, Vol. 10, No. 3 (August 1982), p. 5.

Explain: Why do you think many of the world's women farmers might be called "Invisible Laborers?"[31]

3. Both cassava bread and corn tortillas (the staple foods of much of Latin America) take much preparation time.

    Looking back to the selection on Mayan farmers (in Vol. I, p. 10), what might be one reason that some women in Latin America are not classified as farmers?

4. What things did you notice in the essay about the following groups of women workers in Latin America:

    Single women workers

    Professional women workers

    Domestic servants

    Briefly compare and contrast these Latin American women workers to those in the United States, Europe or Canada.

[31]Susan Hill Gross, *The Invisible Laborers*, (St. Louis Park: Glenhurst Publications, Inc.), 1983.

D. Where From Here?

The great diversity of cultures and the wide variety of geographical areas of Central and South America and the Caribbean means that there is no general agreement about the direction that reforms for women will take. Literacy campaigns in a country like Haiti—where, according to United Nations statistics, only 18% of the women are literate—may take first priority. In some democratic nations like Costa Rica, the major issue may be to increase the number of women who are elected to political offices, while in Paraguay it may be that of having the right to vote. For a woman living in the barrios, or slums, of Lima or Rio de Janiero, the most important issue may be physical survival. For an Argentine woman doctor the issue may be to try to fit home, family and career into her overburdened days. However, Latin American women of all classes do have some common concerns and problems. These include:

- obtaining proper health care for themselves and their children.
- an interest in equal educational opportunities for girls and women.
- working for better communication and understanding between women of various classes.
- the cultural acceptance of machismo and the difficulties this causes women.
- employment opportunities and occupational needs for women.

The following selections briefly describe each of these problems for Latin American women:

Health Care: Lack of proper medical facilities affect both sexes in Latin American, but women face special health problems of getting proper care during pregnancies and for their children. Birth control is a highly controversial issue in many Latin American countries. There is opposition to the encouragement of birth control campaigns from many

Latin American governments, the Roman Catholic Church and from people who feel that industrialized, developed countries are trying to limit the right of poor peoples to have children.[1] However, in some countries like Mexico, one of the leading causes of death in young women is from illegal, often self-induced abortions. It is estimated that of the million or so illegal abortions a year, about 20% lead to serious complications or death for the mother.[2] High infant mortality rates are also a major medical issue in various Latin American countries. The following statistics on infant mortality suggest the problems families—but mothers in particular—have with child care. Issues such as obtaining proper nutrition and medical treatment for their children may still be critical in some areas.[3]

REGION OR COUNTRY	Infant Mortality Rate (deaths to infants under one year of age per 1000)	
	Male	Female
LATIN AMERICA	90	80
MIDDLE AMERICA	76	67
Costa Rica	30	25
El Salvador	56	45
Guatemala	81	71
Honduras	109	97
Mexico	74	66
Nicaragua	128	115
Panama	49	44
CARIBBEAN		
Bahamas	27	23
Barbados	30	24
Cuba	21	22
Dominica	-	-
Dominican Republic	102	90
Grenada	28	19
Haiti	137	123
Jamaica	16	14
Netherland Antilles	-	-
Puerto Rico	23	17
St. Lucia	-	-
Trinidad and Tobago	34	24

[1]Domitilia Barrios de Chugara. *Let Me Speak! Testimony of Domitlia, A Woman of the Bolivian Mines* (New York: Monthly Review Press, 1978), p.198.

[2]Eileen Haley, "The Abortion Struggle in Mexico," *Hecate*, Vol. 7, No. 1 (1981), p. 79.

[3]"World's Women Data Sheet of the Population Reference Bureau, Inc. in Collaboration With UNICEF," April, 1980.

TROPICAL SOUTH AMERICA	104	92
Bolivia	176	159
Brazil	115	103
Colombia	84	71
Ecuador	74	66
Guyana	52	46
Paraguay	67	60
Peru	97	87
Suriname	33	21
Venezuela	50	40
TEMPERATE SOUTH AMERICA	47	41
Argentina	48	42
Chile	42	38
Uruguay	52	49

Education: Besides the lack of proper medical facilities, many areas lack good schools. The following chart gives literacy rates for males/females:[4]

Region or Country	%Enrolled in School, 1975, Ages 6-11, Male Female		%Enrolled in School, 1975 Ages 12-17, Male Female		Percent Adults Literate, Male Female	
MIDDLE AMERICA	84	83	58	46	75	67
Costa Rica	94	95	49	50	89	88
El Salvador	62	63	56	49	-	-
Guatemala	51	49	32	24	54	38
Honduras	67	67	40	39	59	55
Mexico	91	89	62	47	78	70
Nicaragua	54	57	47	48	58	57
Panama	94	95	72	70	79	78
CARIBBEAN	85	87	60	59	67	66
Bahamas	-	-	-	-	90	89
Barbados	-	-	-	-	98	98
Cuba	100	100	67	63	76	80
Dominica	-	-	-	-	58	61
Dominican Republic	75	79	56	56	69	66
Grenada	-	-	-	-	77	76
Haiti	44	34	23	16	29	18
Jamaica	90	58	58	65	79	85
Netherland Antilles	-	-	-	-	93	92
Puerto Rico	100	100	89	94	89	87
St. Lucia	-	-	-	-	51	52
Trinidad and Tobago	96	96	70	64	95	90

[4]*Ibid*.

TROPICAL SOUTH AMERICA	70	72	56	54	74	67
✓ Bolivia	71	63	58	39	75	51
Brazil	69	71	54	52	69	63
Colombia	62	67	54	56	82	80
Ecuador	79	79	56	62	78	70
Guyana	86	86	63	62	91	83
Paraguay	76	76	53	42	85	76
Peru	81	78	80	67	83	62
Suriname	-	-	-	-	84	83
Venezuela	75	74	53	58	80	73
TEMPERATE SOUTH AMERICA	98	98	70	73	93	91
✓Argentina	100	100	61	66	94	92
✓Chile	100	100	85	85	89	87
Uruguay	70	71	72	80	93	94

The chart below compares *illiteracy* rates (note that these are the percentages of people who cannot read and write) in Third World or developing world areas. Compare Latin America's rates with other areas:

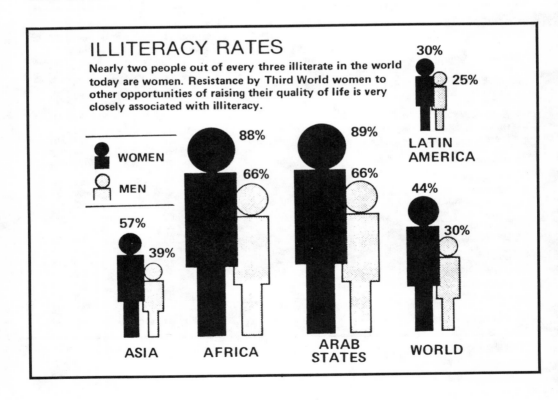

ILLITERACY RATES

Nearly two people out of every three illiterate in the world today are women. Resistance by Third World women to other opportunities of raising their quality of life is very closely associated with illiteracy.

30%
25%

LATIN AMERICA

WOMEN
MEN

ASIA 57% 39%
AFRICA 88% 66%
ARAB STATES 89% 66%
WORLD 44% 30%

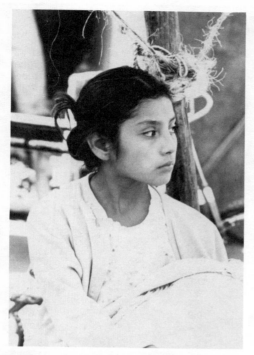

Woman in Oaxaca, Mexico, market

In most areas of Latin America the illiteracy rates for women are somewhat more than those for men. This is one indication that if family income is limited, available resources probably would be used to educate boys in the family rather than girls. A Peruvian woman in the 1970's told of her own father's views on an education for his daughter:

"I would like to study, be a teacher, or a nurse—but my father does not agree. He thinks it's useless to spend money educating women who are going to end up taking care of children and cooking anyway. He says, 'We have to save so your brother can study. When he becomes a professional, he will help you and support you.' And now my brother is an engineer, and I am
still working in the fields, still helping Mama, still taking my crops to market. [5]

Statistics also show that Latin American women in these countries do not attend high schools and colleges at the same rate as men.[6]

When they do attend college, women tend to study what has been considered to be more feminine subjects—to the exclusion of mathematics, engineering and the sciences. One of the major goals of most women's rights groups in Latin America has been to achieve equality in education and to encourage women to enter non-traditional fields of study.

[5]Quoted in, *Latin American Women: The Meek Speak Out*, Jane Turner, ed., (Silver Spring, Maryland: International Educational Development, 1980), p. 49.

[6]Quoted in, Rose Marie Muraro, "Women in Latin America: Phases of Integration," *Amherst Program in Latin American Studies, Occasional Paper Series*, No. 6 (July, 1977), p. 21.

TABLE VIII—SCHOOL ENROLLMENT BY AGE AND LEVEL OF DEVELOPMENT OF COUNTRIES

Countries	Group	Primary enrollment as % of pop. age 7-13	Secondary enrollment as % of pop. age 14-19	Higher educa- tion enrollment as % of pop. age 20-24	Women as % of higher education pop. enrolled
Argentina 72	A	95.0	40.5	17.5	35.8
Uruguay 70	B	95.8	60.8	6.7	45.2
Panama 70	C	93.5	43.0	6.3	46.0
Costa Rica 72	C	101.6	37.8	12.5	37.5
Chile 72	100.0	49.4	9.2 38.3	—	
Venezuela 71	D	83.4	38.6	8.7	34.5
Brazil 71	E	76.2	35.6	6.6	37.0
Mexico 70	E	94.4	24.1	6.1	18.5
Peru 70	E	104.1	39.9	11.0	29.4
Colombia 68	E	62.7	20.5	3.5	26.8
El Salvador 70	F	76.1	19.6	1.5	34.1
Ecuador 69	F	86.7	26.5	6.1	33.1
Paraguay 70	F	92.6	17.6	3.4	40.5
Nicaragua 71	F	76.0	12.7	7.5	19.1
Honduras 70	F	76.7	12.7	7.5	19.1
Guatemala 70	F	49.9	10.9	3.7	17.6
Dominican Republic 70	F	89.3	19.4	4.6	40.1
Bolivia 71	G	84.5	16.0	7.8	28.2
Haiti 68	H	31.0	4.2	0.3	11.2
Cuba 70		103.8	26.8	4.2	—

Class Divisions: Equality in education, discouraged partly by a lack of funds in many Latin American countries for free public education, means that the ability to educate children often depends on the income levels of their families. While some women of the upper classes benefit from the class system, extreme divisions of wealth create financial burdens on the poor. It is estimated in Mexico that about 1% of the nation's population controls about 66% of the national income.[7] Other Latin American countries have similar patterns. In addition, women workers usually are the lowest paid laborers with poor women having little say over the spending of family resources. The following chart gives the percentage of men/women in different income categories in Mexico in 1975, starting with the lowest:[8]

[7]Mary Elmendorf, "Mexico: The Many Worlds of Women," in *Women: Roles and Status in Eight Countries*, Janet Zollinger Giele and Audrey Chapman Smock, eds., (New York: John Wiley, l977), p. 129.

[8]Quoted in, *Latin American and Caribbean Women's Collective Slave of Slaves: The Challenges of Latin American Women* (London: Zed Press, 1977), p. 122.

Economically Active Population by Sex and Monthly Income, 1970 (%)

Income Group (declared incomes in pesos)*	All Activities		Non-Agriculture Activities	
	Men	Women	Men	Women
Up to 499 pesos	44.1	47.7	18.9	45.1
500-999 pesos	27.2	26.6	35.0	27.1
1,000-1,499 pesos	12.6	13.1	20.3	14.0
1,500-2,499 pesos	8.1	8.3	13.2	8.8
2,500-4,999 pesos	5.1	3.5	8.1	3.7
5,000-9,999 pesos	1.9	0.8	3.1	0.8
10,000 pesos and over	1.0	0.6	1.4	0.5
Total	100.0	100.0	100.0	100.0

*Note: 12.50 pesos = $1.00 in 1975.

Source: IX *Censo General de Poblacion*, Mexico: SIC, 1972, from tables 4 and 5 in Gloria Gonzalez Salazar, *La mujer en America latina*, Vol. 1, Mexico: Sepsetentas, 1975.

Male and female agricultural workers in Mexico are paid at about the same rates. In other kinds of employment—even for what is essentially the same work—there are major wage differences between men and women.

Machismo: The cultural concept of machismo has been criticized by both women and men in Latin America because it diminishes respect for women. Some authors have linked machismo to family violence present in Latin America. One woman described such machismo in El Salvadoran men:

"In innumerable ways, the greatest problems of Salvadoran society lie between men and women—not between the political factions of radical and reactionary. Political upheaval, although endemic to our nation, is a sensational release for emotional turmoil that begins in the home. Men subconsciously seek physical violence as an answer to all problems, whether they be in the streets, against their political opposition, or with their wives and children. Violence and inhumanity in our country has become a way of life.

"Life is especially difficult for our rural women. Living conditions are extremely harsh. Health and nutrition are only as good as the quality of the water, food, and sanitary facilities, all of which range from poor to non-existent. All the good land for farming is owned and operated by a small oligarchy that is politically committed to keeping things just as they are. With so little of the land available to the small farmer, the rural people are dependent on the mercy of the landed few. Because of this, men who earn little or no income have almost nothing to be proud of except their virility. They have few ways to relieve their frustrations, so women often bear the brunt of their discontents.

"There is absolutely no respect for the human dignity of women. It is common for their husbands and fathers to beat, kick and humiliate them in the most vulgar ways. They act ashamed to be seen in public with their wives, sisters or mothers, as if it would make them seem less manly among their friends. Much of the Salvadoran man's free time is

133

spent competing with his cronies for the attentions of casual girlfriends to prove their masculinity. The tragic results are unwanted, illegitimate children.

"The majority of men in our rural communities refer to women as 'idiots,' 'pigs,' 'worthless,' 'disobedient,' 'deceitful,' 'disloyal,' 'lazy,' and 'stupid.' A man most often thinks of his wife as an expensive burden because she eats and consumes food that would otherwise be his. If it suits his mood, any of the above perceived qualities serve as sufficient reason for him to mistreat his wife."[9]

Not all Latin American societies tolerate this kind of physical and verbal abuse of women. But in some areas, particularly where alcoholism is a problem, family violence is frequent.[10] In a study of Brazilian women who ended marital unions, it was found that over half did so because of physical abuse.[11] Latin America is not unique in having alcoholism and violence as part of its family patterns, but the concept of machismo and the cultural emphasis on the father as head of the family does provide a setting that encourages it. This pattern of family violence has been difficult to break.

Employment Needs: One of the reasons women are willing to remain in violent relationships is their lack of economic alternatives. Though single women can find work as domestic servants, most employers do not want servants who have children. There are still few factory jobs, and women with dependents have difficulty competing for jobs with single women because single women have fewer home responsibilities and so can work for lower wages. With generally less education than men, women may have few job possibilities open to them. Development programs of Latin American governments or United States foreign aid programs often include training for men, but not for women. When women are employed outside the home, they are often expected to do double duty—fulfilling both their wage job at their work place and domestic chores and child care at home.

For some Latin American women, these issues may not be major ones. They live comfortably and are content within their cultural boundaries. But for others, these are serious problems which affect not only themselves as Latin American women, but also the direction in which Latin American countries will take in the future.

Venezuela recently adopted constitutional reforms including Article 61 that calls for *"el principio de la igualad de todos los venezolanos"—"the principle that all Venezuelans are equal."*

---

[9]Ana Audilia Moreira de Campos, "Our National Inferiority Complex: A Cause for Violence?" in Turner, p. 66-67. Reprinted with permission of June Haney Turner and International Educational Development, Inc. from the article, "Our National Inferiority Complex: A Cause for Violence?" by Ana Audilia Moreira de Campos, El Salvador, in *Latin American Woman: The Meek Speak Out*, edited by June H. Turner. Copyright ©1980 by June Haney Turner and International Educational Development, Inc.

[10]Susan C. Bourque and Kay Barbara Warren, *Women of the Andes* (Ann Arbor: The University of Michigan Press, 1981), p. 107.

[11]Heleieth Saffioti, "Relationships of Sex and Social Class in Brazil," in *Sex and Class in Latin America*, Jane Nash and Helen Icken Safa, eds., (New York: Praeger, 1976), p. 158.

This means that Venezuelan women have the legal power of an Equal Rights Amendment to demand the elimination of discrimination against them. One concern expressed was whether this new constitutional reform might not *"destruir La Unidad de la Familia"*—*"destroy family unity."* Those answering this concern did so in the following way:

"No, todo lo contrario. Un Código Civil sin discriminaciones, puede ayudar a crear en la familia relaciones mas francas, justas e igualitarias."

("No, completely the contrary. A civil code without discrimination, helps to create in family relations more frankness, justice and equality.")

"Una verdadera democracia social se sustenta sobre una verdadera democracia familiar."

("A true democratic society is maintained by a truly democratic family.")

Mercedes Pulido, head of the Venezuelan ministry which aids women to become participants in economic development, commented on these constitutional changes:

"La Democracia descansa sobre la igualdad plena de sus ciudadanos como instrumento para la libertad y responsabilidad."

("The Democracy that rests upon the complete equality of its citizens becomes an instrument for liberty and responsibility.")[12]

The future of women in the more than 30 countries of Latin America depends on many factors. The articles in this book make it clear that women of Latin America have pursued and succeeded in many areas of life. They have been field and mine workers, writers, philosophers and politicians. They

Mercedes Pulido, sponsor of the Venezuelan constitutional reform giving women equal legal rights.

have fought in wars of independence and demonstrated against political regimes. Although their life conditions have varied greatly, they have been distinguished by their determination and bravery.

★　　★　　★

---

[12]Ana Hirsz, *Derecho A La Ignaldad*, Publicaciones Populares de CESAP: Centro al Servicio de la Accion Popular y CONSUCRE, Concejo Municipal del Distrito Sucre. Petare. (August, 1981), p. 26, p. 3.

Points to Consider

A Summary

Step 1
Several categories of problems are mentioned in this selection. Look back over these five categories and below each one, list the things you see as needing the most change within that category.
Health Care:
Education:
Class Divisions:
Machismo:
Employment Needs:

Step 2
Look over your list of sub-problems under the five categories. Suggest a possible solution to each one.

Step 3
Think back over this book and for each of your solutions decide whether they would be solutions that most Latin Americans would be willing to adopt or which they would probably reject. Keep in mind the following cultural realities of Latin America:

Economic:
Most are classified as Third World or Developing—most are poorer nations.

Social Arrangements:
The importance of the family and machismo/ marianismo cultural concepts and the strong class system.

Political:
Latin America has had few democracies, several repressive military regimes as well as dictatorships of the left—such as Castro's Cuba. Many areas of Latin America have been known for political instability.

Education:
The members of the upper classes had best access to an education; institutions for good higher education and private schools have been available to them. Generally, little money was set aside for public education.

Religion:
The Roman Catholic Church has been dominant in all of Latin America.

Art:
Strong literary and artistic traditions are present. Women are especially prominent as poets and novelists.

Defend the decisions you made by briefly explaining why you feel that certain solutions would be *rejected* and certain ones *accepted*.

Step 4
Write two summary paragraphs of about 200-300 words on what you see as two *major problems* for Latin American women and the *major strengths* of Latin American societies to overcome these problems.

WOMEN IN LATIN AMERICA
SELECTED BIBLIOGRAPHY

Anton, Ferdinand. *Women in Pre-Colombian America*. New York: Abner Schram, 1973.

Barrios, Domitila de Chungara. *Let Me Speak! Testimony of Domitila, a Woman of the Bolivian Mines*. New York: Monthly Review, 1978.

Bourgue, Susan and Kay Barbara Warren. *Women of the Andes*. Ann Arbor: University of Michigan, 1981.

Boxer, C. R. *Women in Iberian Expansion Overseas 1415-1815*. Cambridge: Oxford University Press, 1975.

Bronstein, Audrey. *The Triple Struggle: Latin American Peasant Women*. Boston: South End Press, 1983.

Elmendorf, Mary Lindsay. *Nine Mayan Women*. New York: Schenkman Publishers, 1976.

Fraser, Nicholas and Marysa Navarro. *Eva Perón*. New York: W. W. Norton, 1980.

Hahner, June E. *Women in Latin American History*. Los Angeles: UCLA Latin American Center, 1976.

Henderson, James and Linda. *Ten Notable Women of Latin America*. Chicago: Nelson Hall, 1978.

Knaster, Meri. *Women in Spanish America: Annotated Bibliography*. Boston: G. K. Hall, 1977.

Latin American and Caribbean Women's Collective. *Slaves of Slaves: The Challenge of Latin American Women*. London: Zed Press, 1980.

Lavrin, A. *Latin American Women*. Westport, Greenwood Press, 1978.

Lewis, Oscar. *Four Women: Living the Revolution, An Oral History of Contemporary Cuba*. Urbana: University of Illinois Press, 1977.

Macias, Anna. *Against All Odds: The Feminist Movement in Mexico to 1940*. Westport: Greenwood Press, 1982.

Martin, Luis. *Daughters of the Conquistadores*. Albuquerque: University of New Mexico Press, 1983.

Martinez-Alier, Verena. *Marriage, Class and Colour in 19th Century Cuba: A Study of Racial Attitudes and Sexual Values in a Slave Society*. New York: Cambridge University Press, 1974.

Mathurin, Lucille. *The Rebel Woman in the British West Indies During Slavery*. Jamaica: Kingston Institute of Jamaica, 1975.

May, Stella. *Men, Maidens and Mantillas: Changing Role of Women in Latin America*. Bowling Green: Gordon Press, 1976.

Montgomery, Paul. *Eva, Evita: The Life and Death of Eva Perón*. New York: Simon & Schuster, 1979.

Murphy, Yolanda and Robert. *Women of the Forest*. New York: Columbia University Press, 1974.

Nash, June. *Sex and Class in Latin America*. New York: Praeger, 1976.

Pescatello, Ann. *Female and Male in Latin America: Essays*. Pittsburgh: University of Pittsburgh Press, 1973.

Randall, Margaret. *Cuban Women Now*. Toronto: Women's Press, 1974.

Roberts, George. *Women in Jamaica*. Millwood, N.Y.: Kraus, 1977.

Saulniers, Suzanne Smith and Cathy A. Rakowski. *Women in the Development Process: A Select Bibliography on Women in Sub-Saharan Africa and Latin America*. Austin, Institute of Latin American Studies, 1977.

Slater, Mariam. *The Caribbean Family*. New York: St. Martin's Press, 1977.

Taylor, J. M. *Eva Perón: The Myths of a Woman*. Chicago: University of Chicago Press, 1979.

Turner, June, ed., *Latin American Woman: The Meek Speak Out*. Silver Spring: International Educational Development, 1980.

Youssef, Nadia H. *Women and Work in Developing Societies. Population Monograph Series*, No. 15. Berkeley: University of California Institute of International Studies, 1974.

Glossary

Abbess: A woman who is the Superior or leader of a convent of nuns.

Amazons: Ancient accounts (c. 400 B.C.) reveal tales of female warriors in the Black Sea area near the Soviet Union. Women soldiers of Dahomey (Benin) in Africa were called Amazons. In Latin America there were various stories of tribes of women warriors or Amazons for which the river in Brazil was named.

Andean: A person who comes from the area of the Andes mountains in South America, usually of indigenous American ancestry.

Anthropology (Anthropologist):   The branch of social science that deals with cultural development and social customs of people. Anthropologists often study small groups of people to observe their social organizations.

Archaeology (Archaeologist):   The science of studying prehistoric or historic peoples by analyzing their artifacts and other remains. Often involves excavation or digging up these remains at the site of an ancient (or more recent) society. The science of excavation of sites.

Artifacts: Any object made by a human being. Frequently associated with finds at archaeological digs.

Autocrat/ Autocratic: An absolute ruler; monarchs who act on the belief that there are no restrictions on the use of their power—except perhaps by God.

Bishop: A church priest or minister of higher rank who supervises a number of churches.

Black Carib: People who live along the coast of northeastern South America of African descent but who speak a Native Caribbean language.

Cassava/Manioc: Tropical plants of several varieties, cultivated for their roots and made into a kind of bread or meal.

Chronicler: A person who writes day-to-day records of events.

Clergy: The group of people trained in a religion and authorized to conduct worship for that religion.

Codex: Early, often ancient books made by stitching together sheets of paper. In the case of those of Maya and Aztec codices, they folded out as does an accordian.

Concubine (Concubinage):   A secondary wife who has some of the rights and privileges of a wife but less status than a regular wife.

Conquistador: (plural, conquistadors/in Spanish, conquistadores)	Spanish soldiers of the 16th century who conquered Mexico, Peru and other parts of what is now Latin America.
Convent/ Monastery:	A dwelling occupied by a community of people living under the same religious vows while separated from other people. Convents are occupied by nuns. The term monasteries is usually used to refer to monks.
Creole:	A person born in the Americas but whose ancestors are "Peninsulars" from Europe, usually Spain and/or Portugal.
(The) Crown:	Means in these essays the Royal rulers of Spain or Portugal.
Dirge:	A funeral song or tune, one that expresses mourning in order to honor the dead.
Divine right of monarchs:	The belief that God gave queens and kings the right to rule their people.
Dowry:	The payment in money, goods or land which a woman gives to her husband at their marriage.
Elite:	People who belong to a high class or rank.
Friar:	A man who has taken vows that commit his life to the Catholic religious community known as the mendicant order. Friars do not live in monasteries and/or own community property.
Hierarchy:	An order by rank such as the one in the Roman Catholic Church where the order might have been from priest, bishop, archbishop, cardinal and pope—with the parish priest at the bottom and the pope at the tope of the ranking.
Hieroglyphics:	A type of writing where pictures are used as words. The pictures are simplified drawings of things they represent.
Hispanic:	A Spanish speaking country or person.
Iberian Peninsula/ Iberia:	Spain and Portugal together are called a peninsula because they have water on three sides.
Indians:	The name European explorers gave Native Americans when they first landed on the American continents. The explorers believed they were in India.
Indigenous Americans/ Indigenous Peoples:	Any people of the many groups that occupied areas of the Americas before the conquests by the Spanish, Portuguese and other Europeans. Sometimes called Native Americans and, inaccurately, Indians.

Inquisition:	An investigation by an authority—usually for religious or political reasons—often characterized by its prejudiced investigators, cruel punishments and lack of respect for individual rights.
Islam:	Religious faith of the Muslims based on the teachings of Muhammad and the belief in one god, Allah.
Latin America:	Areas of Central, South America and the West Indies where Spanish, Portuguese and French languages are the major ones spoken.
Matriarchy:	Societies in which the mother is usually head of household with descent lines traced through the mother.
Midwife:	A woman who helps other women in childbirth. She often used folk remedies and wisdom gained through experience.
Monarchy:	A government having an absolute ruler (such as queen or king), usually hereditary and keeping the position for life.
Monastery:	A place where monks or nuns went to live a particularly spiritual life under religious vows. In modern times this term usually means a religious retreat for monks while the term convent is used for nuns.
Monks:	Males under religious vows who try to live an especially spiritual existence within monasteries.
Machismo:	A cultural ideal common in Latin America. A masculine code where men are to be personally brave, protective of family (especially women) able to operate effectively in the outside world and are usually quick to take insult.
Marianismo:	A cultural ideal common in Latin America. A feminine code where women are to be religious and pious, focused on family, secluded at home, and the moral force of their families.
Monogamous:	The practice of being married to only one person at a time.
Mulatto:	A person who has one white parent and one black parent.
Muslim (or Moslem):	People who follow the religious teaching of Muhammad. Their religion is called Islam and they believe in one god, Allah.
Natal (family):	The family of one's birth.
New Spain:	The land Spain claimed in the American continents. At one time included all of South America (except Brazil), Central America, Mexico, much of the West Indies, Florida and much of the land in the United States west of the Mississippi.

New World/ Old World:	*New World*—The name given to North and South America and their islands by Europeans. Probably the first groups of Europeans to discover the existence of the Americas were in the 15th century. *Old World*—The name Europeans gave to the world as they knew it after discovering the American continents.
Novice:	A person who has been received into a religious community for a period of probation before taking final vows.
Nun/Nunnery:	A woman who takes religious vows to try to live an especially holy or spiritual life. A nunnery is a place where nuns live, often separated from the secular world (see also convent, secular).
Oligarchy:	Rule by a small group of people or rule by a small elite.
Patois:	A mixture of two or more languages spoken as the ordinary language of a people.
Patriarchy:	Societies where the father is usually head of household, and descent lines are traced through the father.
Patron:	Usually refers to a person who supports an artist or writer with money.
Peninsular:	The highest class (or caste) of Latin Americans after the conquest. They had been born in Spain (or Portugal) and so were from the Iberian Peninsula.
Plantain:	A type of banana which is usually cooked before being eaten.
Polygyny:	The practice of a man having more than one wife at a time.
Postern:	A back door or gate; private entrance.
Pre-Columbian:	Belonging to the period before Columbus explored the Americas.
Prelate:	A person of high rank in the Roman Catholic Church (archbishop, bishop, etc.).
Priest:	In the Roman Catholic Church, an ordained man whose job is to conduct religious worship and religious ceremonies as well as other activities for a Church.
Quartermaster Corps:	Branch of an army that provides clothing and food for the troops.
Regent:	One who serves as a monarch until the rightful queen or king comes of age. Frequently the mother of a prince.
Relief (in art):	A carving where the figures rise up slightly from a flat background.

Seclusion: To be kept (or to keep oneself) with a special group and away from other people. Women in some societies have been secluded or kept away from men and the public world.

Secular: Things of this world in contrast to spiritual or eternal concerns.

Sor: Spanish title meaning "Sister"—referring to a nun of the Roman Catholic faith.

Staple: A basic food that people depend on for their day-to-day nutrition.

Suffrage: Refers here to the right to vote (or to be given 'the franchise').

Treason: The crime of making war against one's country or helping one's country's enemies.

Viceroy: A person appointed to rule a country or area as a deputy of a queen or king (Spain in this case).

Virgin of Guadalupe: Patron Saint of Mexico.

Yucatan: The peninsula that forms the southern part of Mexico where the Mayan civilization flourished.

ABOUT THE AUTHORS

Marjorie Wall Bingham was born in St. Paul, Nebraska, received a B.A. degree from Grinnell College and M.A. and Ph.D. degrees from the University of Minnesota. She has taught high school history for the St. Louis Park school system since 1963. Dr. Bingham's experience also includes teaching in a junior high school in Davenport, Iowa, and at the University of Minnesota. She is presently co-director of WWAS (Women in World Area Studies) and has served as a member of the Minnesota Council for the Social Studies Executive Board and as president of WHOM (Women Historians of the Midwest). Presently she is a board member of the teaching division of The American Historical Association and serves on The Minnesota Sex Equity Board of the Minnesota Department of Education.

Susan Hill Gross was born in Minneapolis, Minnesota, and received her B.A. degree from the University of Minnesota and her M.A. degree in history from the College of William and Mary. Ms. Gross taught secondary English and history in Denbigh, Virginia; Savannah, Georgia; and the Robbinsdale Schools in Minnesota before becoming a director of the curriculum project Women in World Area Studies. She has also taught at the University of Minnesota and presently serves as president of WHOM (Women Historians of the Midwest). She is currently director of the Upper Midwest Women's History Center for Teachers.

Dr. Bingham and Ms. Gross are frequently invited to lecture to various educational and community groups on issues concerning women's history, integrating women's studies into the curriculum and on issues concerning Title IX.

The activity which is the subject of this book was supported in whole or in part by the Northwest Area Foundation and the St. Louis Park and Robbinsdale Schools. However, the opinions expressed herein do not necessarily reflect the position or policy of the Northwest Area Foundation or the School Districts #283 or #281, and no official endorsement should be inferred.

Authors' Acknowledgments

The project *Women in World Area Studies* began with the support of two Minneapolis suburban school districts—St. Louis Park and Robbinsdale. The project was funded by the Elementary and Secondary Education Act, Title IV-C for three years. The Northwest Area Foundation funded three additional units on women in Africa, Latin America and Japan.

We would particularly like to thank the following administrators, teachers, editors, consultants and friends who made possible this curriculum unit on *Women in Latin America*:

Michael E. Hickey, Superintendent, and Jim Gavenda of the St. Louis Park Schools.

Mary H. Rojas, Director of Women in Development, Virginia Polytechnic Institute, and Howard Shorr, Los Angeles Schools, who acted as readers for this unit and who made suggestions for changes in the manuscript.

Alyce Fuller who provided secretarial skills, suggestions about readability of the text and organized the permissions for the photographs and quoted materials.

Eileen Soderberg who read the text, contributed her typing skills, time and, not incidentally, her safekeeping of the manuscript.

DeAnna DuBois, Andres Himmelstrup and Marian Iverson who donated excellent photographs used in both the book and sound filmstrip.

The University of Minnesota library staff that made possible the research for the series of books of which *Women in Latin America* is a part.

Finally, our husbands, Bert Gross and Thomas Egan who assisted us by proofreading the manuscript and by understanding the time involved in this curriculum project.